101 COUNTRY HITS FOR BUSKERS

Piano/Organ Edition with Guitar Chords.

GW00373233

Wise Publications London/New York/Sydney

101 COUNTRY HITS FOR BUSKERS

Exclusive Distributors:
Music Sales Limited 8/9 Frith Street, London W1V 5TZ, England.
Music Sales Corporation 257 Park Avenue South, New York, NY10010, U.S.A.
Music Sales Pty. Limited 120 Rothschild Avenue, Rosebery, NSW 2018, Australia

This book © Copyright 1984 by Wise Publications
ISBN 0.7119.0346.8 Order No. AM 33680

Art direction by Mike Bell. Cover illustration by Graham Thompson. Compiled by Peter Evans.

Music Sales complete catalogue lists thousands of titles and
is free from your local music book shop, or direct from Music Sales Limited.
Please send a cheque or Postal order for £1.50 for postage to
Music Sales Limited, 8/9 Frith Street, London W1V 5TZ.

C SHUFFLE 1
T 125
M3

1
Act Naturally

Music **Johnny Russell**
Words **Vonnie Morrison**

Moderato

They're gon-na put me in the mov-ies, _____
hope _____ you come and see me in my mov-ies, _____

They're gon-na make a big star out of me.
then I know that you will plain-ly see.

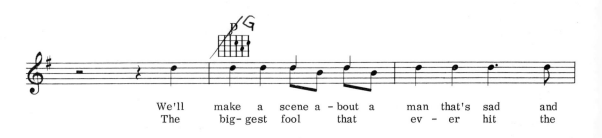

We'll make a scene a-bout a man that's sad and
The big-gest fool that ev-er hit the

lone - ly, _____
big time, _____
And all I got-ta do is

al Coda

act nat - ural-ly. Well, I'll bet you I'm

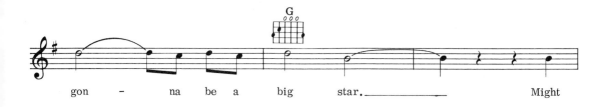

gon - na be a big star._____ Might

win an Os - car, you can't nev-er tell; The

mov-ies____ are gon - na make me a big star,_____

___ 'Cause I can play the part so well.____

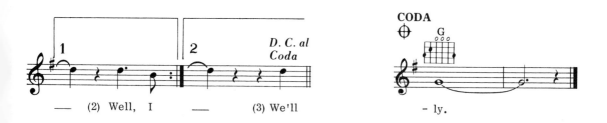

— (2) Well, I — (3) We'll - ly.

3. We'll make a scene about a man that's sad and lonely,
   And beggin' down upon his bended knee;
   I'll play the part, but I won't need rehearsin',
   'Cause all I have to do is act naturally.

All I Ever Need Is You

Words & Music **Jimmy Holiday & Eddie Reeves**

EASY LISTENING
S/J ORCH/SWING 84

(Hey, Won't You Play) Another Somebody Done Somebody Wrong Song

Words & Music **Larry Butler & Chips Moman**

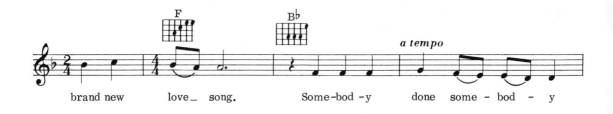

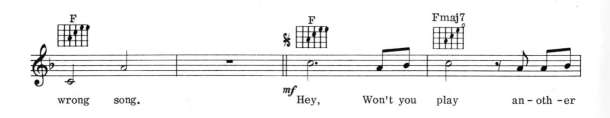

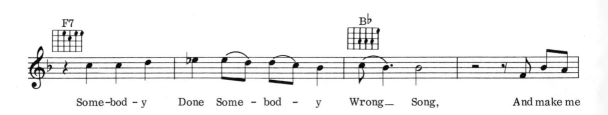

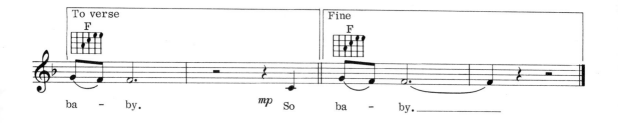

ba - by.   *mp* So ba - by._____

VERSE

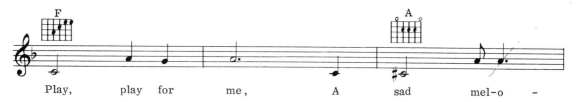

Play,   play for   me,   A   sad   mel-o -

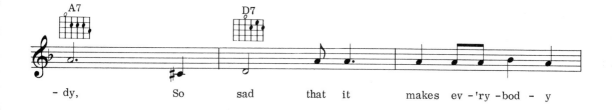

- dy,   So   sad   that   it   makes ev -'ry-bod - y

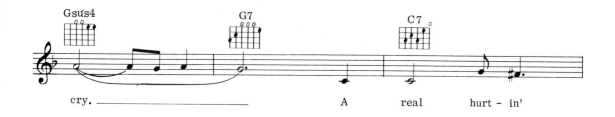

cry. _____   A   real   hurt - in'

song,   A - bout a   love   that's gone___   wrong,   'Cause

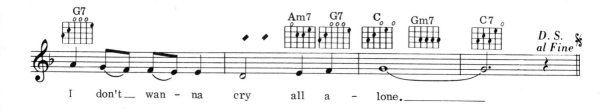

I don't__ wan - na   cry   all   a - lone._____

4
Annie's Song

Words & Music **John Denver**

5
Bad, Bad Leroy Brown

Words & Music **Jim Croce**

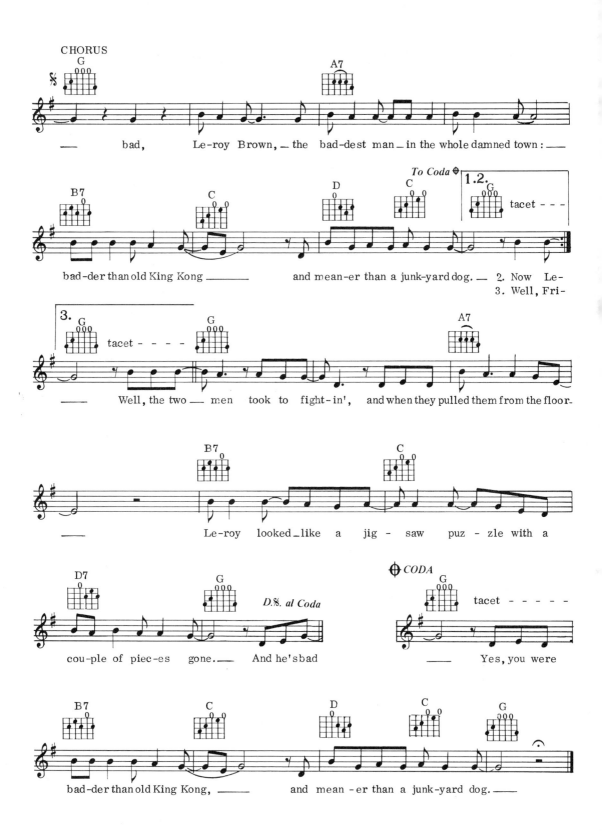

6
Banks Of The Ohio

Traditional

I asked my love to take a walk, —
knife a-gainst his breast —
home 'tween twelve and one, —

To take a walk, — just a lit-tle walk, —
as in-to my arms he pressed —
I cried, "My God, — what have I done! —

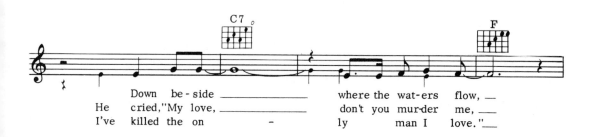

Down be-side where the wat-ers flow, —
He cried, "My love, don't you mur-der me, —
I've killed the on - ly man I love." —

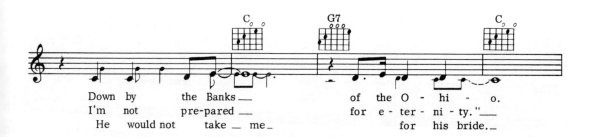

Down by the Banks of the O - hi - o.
I'm not pre-pared for e-ter-ni-ty."
He would not take me for his bride.

And on - ly say   that you'll be mine, ＿   In no

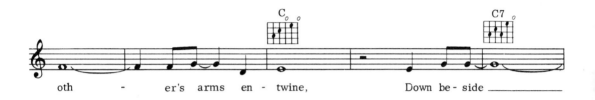

oth — er's arms en - twine,   Down be - side ＿＿＿＿

＿ where the wa-ters flow ＿   Down by the Banks ＿
[Where the wa-ters flow   ]

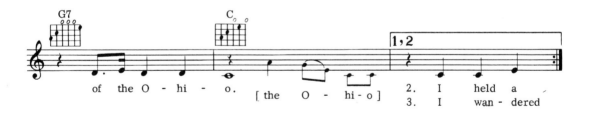

of the O - hi - o.   [the   O - hi - o]   2. I   held a
3. I   wan - dered

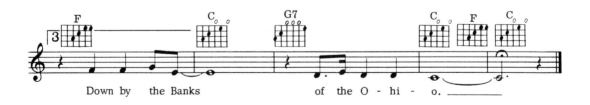

Down by the Banks   of the O - hi - o. ＿＿＿＿

Better Love Next Time

Words & Music **Steve Pippin, Johnny Slate & Larry Keith**

I'm your friend__ you can
Some-times it's bet-ter to

talk to me.__ I read your face, I see __ mis-er-y. __
let it all go. __ I've been there __ and I think I should know. __

'Cause the one you love _____ has left you dry. __
So have a good cry _____ wash out your heart. __

Don't start be-liev-in' that you're gon-na die. _____ Just
If you keep it in-side it-'ll tear _____ you a-part.

pick your heart up off __ the floor _____ and
Some-times you lose__ but you're gon - na win _____ if you

8
Blanket On The Ground

Words & Music **R. Bowling**

Blue Moon Of Kentucky

Words & Music **Bill Monroe**

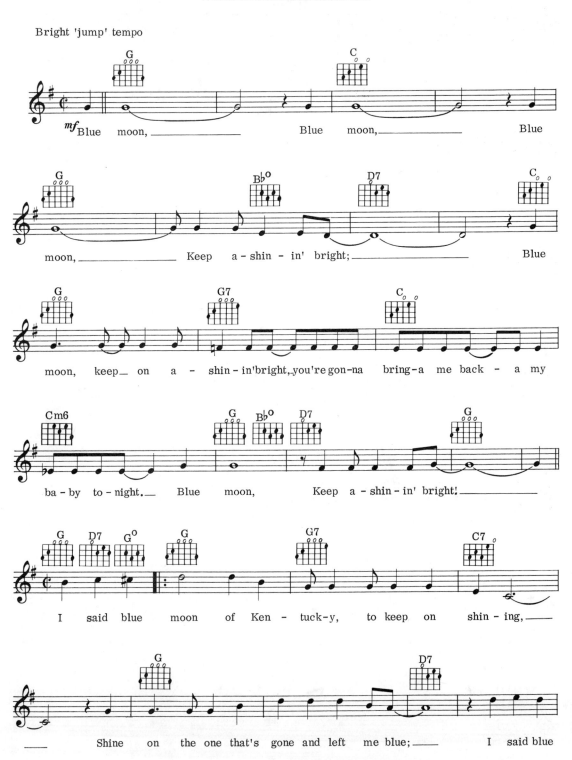

10
Born To Lose

Words & Music **Ted Daffan**

Moderato

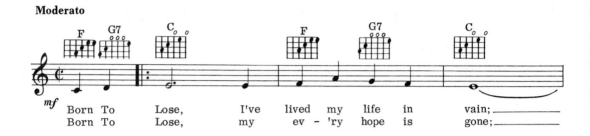

Born To Lose, I've lived my life in vain;____
Born To Lose, my ev - 'ry hope is gone;____

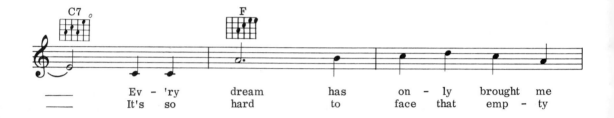

____ Ev - 'ry dream has on - ly brought me
____ It's so hard to face that emp - ty

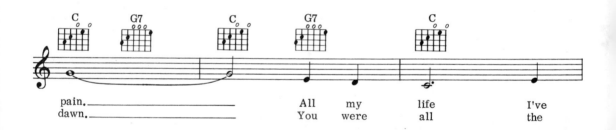

pain._____ All my life I've
dawn._____ You were all the

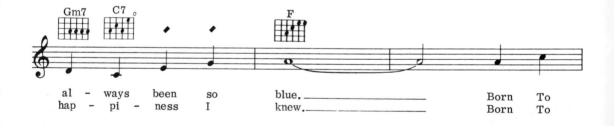

al - ways been so blue._____ Born To
hap - pi - ness I knew._____ Born To

Lose and now I'm los - in' you._____
Lose and now I'm los - in' you._____

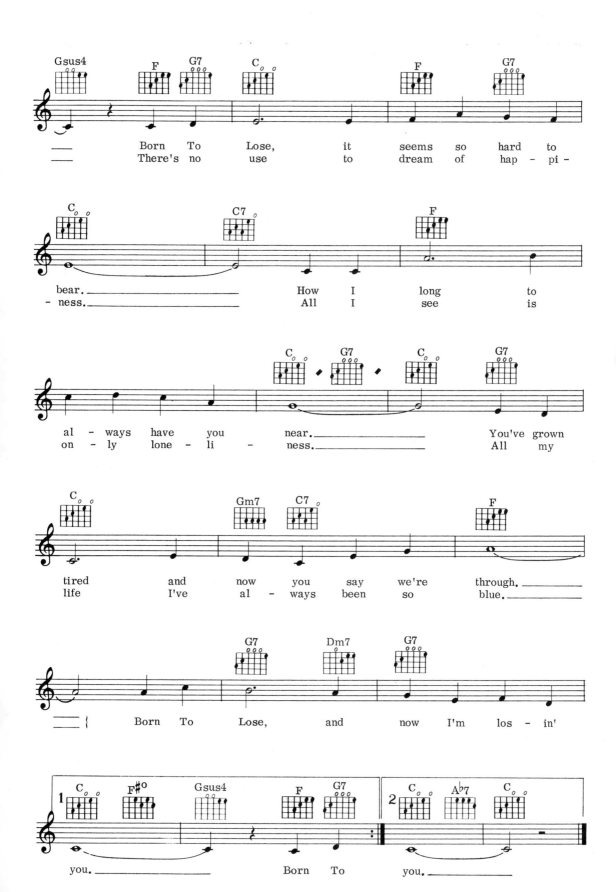

Busted

Words & Music **Harlan Howard**

SINGER SONG
CALI COUNTRY T R2

NEW COUNTRY
MC.

In a lazy style

My bills are all due and the ba - by needs shoes and I'm bus -ted,_____
Went to my bro-ther to ask for a loan, I was bus -ted,_____

_____ Cot-ton is down to a quarter of a pound, but I'm
I hate to beg like a dog with-out its bone, but I'm

bus -ted._____ I've got a cow that went dry, And a
bus -ted._____ My___ bro - ther said there ain't a

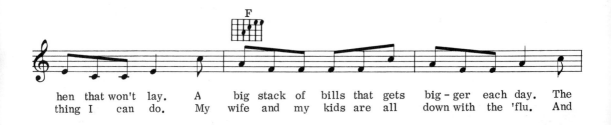

hen that won't lay. A big stack of bills that gets big - ger each day. The
thing I can do. My wife and my kids are all down with the 'flu. And

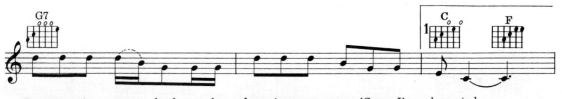

Coun -ty is gon-na haul my be - long-ings a - way, 'Cause I'm bus -ted.
I was just think - ing a - bout call-ing on you, 'Cause I'm

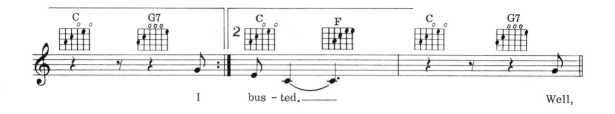

I bus-ted._____ Well,

I am no thief, but a man can go wrong When he's bus-ted._____

_____ The food that we canned___ last sum-mer is gone, and I'm

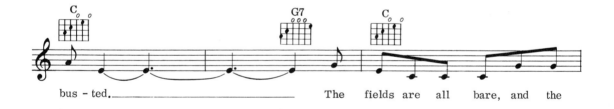

bus-ted._____ The fields are all bare, and the

cot-ton won't grow. Me and my fam-'ly got to pack up and go, But

I'll make a liv-ing, just where I don't know, 'Cause I'm bus-ted._____

PICKIN' SWING T167

12
Chantilly Lace

Words & Music **J.P. Richardson**

(Ha - ha-ha - ha - ha)   Oh, you sweet thing!

Do I what?

Will I what?   Oh,

Baby, you know what I like!

(no chord) C7

f *mp* Chan - til - ly Lace___ and a pret - ty face,___ and a pon - y tail___

F C7

___ hang-in' down, ___ Wig-gle in her walk and a gig-gle in her

F F7

talk. Makes the world go 'round, _____ Ain't

B♭ F

noth - in' in this world like a big eyed girl___ to make me act so fun-ny, make me

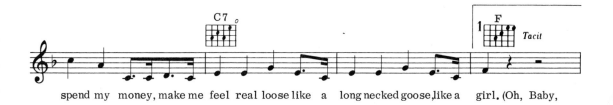

C7 1. F *Tacit*

spend my money, make me feel real loose like a long necked goose, like a girl. (Oh, Baby,

2. F

mf *f*

that's-a what I like.) girl. (Oh, Baby, that's-a what I like.)

6/8 SLOW ROCK   BALLADS MC
T10

13
Can't Help Falling In Love

Words & Music George Weiss, Hugo Peretti & Luigi Creatore

Coat Of Many Colours

Words & Music **Dolly Parton**

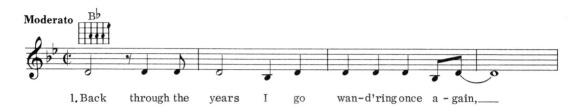

1. Back through the years I go wan-d'ring once a-gain,___

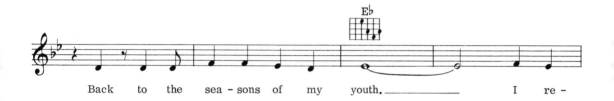

Back to the sea-sons of my youth.___ I re-

-call a box of rags that some-one gave us, And

how my ma-ma put the rags___ to use.___ There were

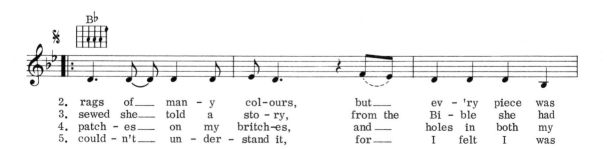

2. rags of___ man-y col-ours, but___ ev-'ry piece was
3. sewed she___ told a sto-ry, from the Bi-ble she had
4. patch-es___ on my britch-es, and___ holes in both my
5. could-n't___ un-der-stand it, for___ I felt I was

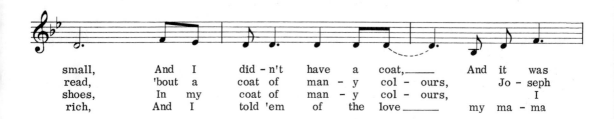

small,   And   I   did-n't   have   a   coat,_____   And   it   was
read,   'bout   a   coat   of   man - y   col - ours,   Jo - seph
shoes,   In   my   coat   of   man - y   col - ours,   I
rich,   And   I   told 'em   of   the   love_____   my   ma - ma

way   down   in   the   fall. _____   Ma - ma   sewed   the   rags   to -
wore   and   then   she   said, _____   Per - haps   this coat   will
hur - ried   off   to   school,____   Just   to   find   the oth - ers
sewed   in   ev - 'ry   stitch,_____   And   I   told   them all   the

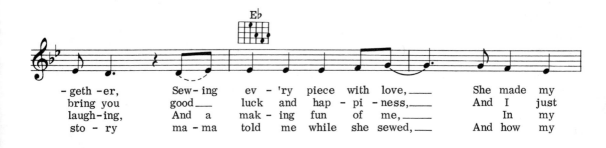

- geth -er,   Sew- ing   ev - 'ry   piece   with   love, ____   She made   my
bring you   good____   luck   and hap - pi - ness,____   And   I   just
laugh-ing,   And   a   mak - ing   fun   of   me, ____   In   my
sto - ry   ma - ma   told   me   while   she   sewed, ___   And how   my

coat   of   man-y   col - ours   that   I   was   so   proud of._____
could-n't wait to   wear it,   Ma- ma blessed it   with   a   kiss._____
coat   of   man-y   col - ours   my   ma - ma made   for   me._____
coat   of   man-y   col - ours   was worth   more   than all   their clothes._____

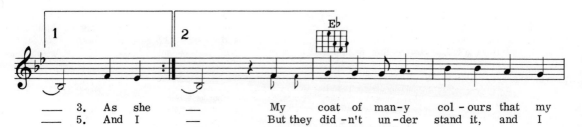

____ 3. As she   ____   My   coat   of man-y   col - ours   that   my
____ 5. And I   ____   But they did -n't un-der stand it,   and   I

14
Coat Of Many Colours

Words & Music **Dolly Parton**

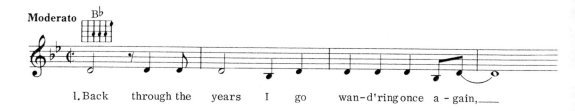

1. Back through the years I go wan-d'ring once a-gain,___

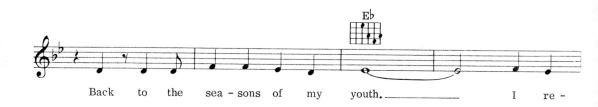

Back to the sea-sons of my youth.___ I re-

-call a box of rags that some-one gave us, And

how my ma-ma put the rags___ to use.___ There were

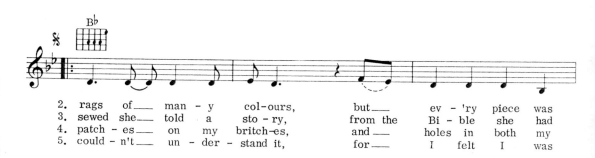

2. rags of___ man-y col-ours, but___ ev-'ry piece was
3. sewed she___ told a sto-ry, from the Bi-ble she had
4. patch-es___ on my britch-es, and___ holes in both my
5. could-n't___ un-der-stand it, for___ I felt I was

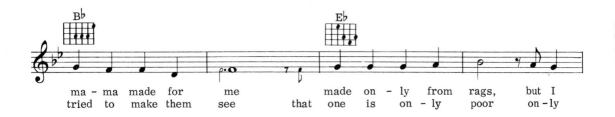

ma - ma made for me made on - ly from rags, but I
tried to make them see that one is on - ly poor on - ly

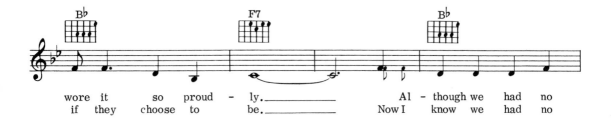

wore it so proud - ly._____ Al - though we had no
if they choose to be._____ Now I know we had no

mon - ey, I was rich as I could be, In my coat of man-y
mon - ey, but I was rich as I could be, In my coat of man-y

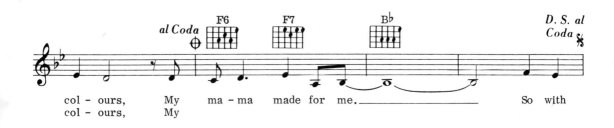

al Coda   D. S. al Coda

col - ours, My ma - ma made for me._____ So with
col - ours, My

CODA

Ma - ma made_ for me._____ She made for me._____

15
Country Bumpkin

Words & Music **Don Wayne**

He walked in - to the bar and placed his lank - y frame up
bar - room girl with wise and know - ing eyes slow - ly

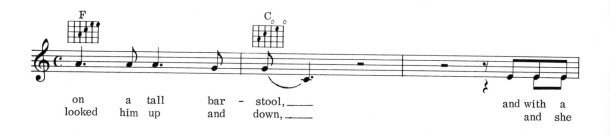

on a tall bar - stool,_____ and with a
looked him up and down,_____ and she

long, soft south - ern drawl said "I'll just have a glass of an - y - thing that's
thought "I won - der how on earth that Coun - try Bump - king found his way to

cool.
A town."

And she said "Hel-lo Coun-try Bump-kin', How's the frost out on the

pump-kins?_____ I've seen some sights, but man, you're some-thing.___

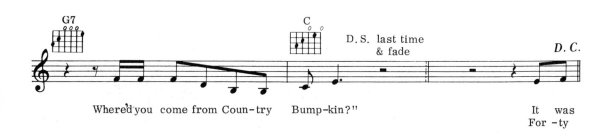

Where'd you come from Coun-try Bump-kin?"

It was
For -ty

Just a short year later in a sweat—drenched bed of joy and tears and death—like pain,
Into this wondrous world of many wonders, one more wonder came.
That same woman's face was wrapped up in a raptured look of love and tenderness,
As she marvelled at the soft and warm and cuddly boy—child feeding at her breast.
CHORUS: And she said "Hello, Country Bumpkin, fresh as frost out on the pumpkins;
        I've seen some sights, but babe, you're somethin',
        Mama loves her Country Bumpkin."

Forty years of hard work later, in a simple quiet and peaceful country place,
The heavy hand of time had not erased the raptured wonder from the woman's face.
She was lying on her death bed knowing fully well her race was nearly run,
But she softly smiled and looked into the sad eyes of her husband and her son.
CHORUS: And she said "So long, Country Bumpkins, the frost is gone now from the pumpkins.
        I've seen some sights, and life's been somethin',
        See you later, Country Bumpkins."

16
Cut Across Shorty

Words & Music **Marijohn Wilkin & Wayne P. Walker**

Bright and rhythmic

1. A coun-try boy named Short-y, And a ci-ty boy named
2. Dan with his long legs fly-in', Left___ Short-y far be-
3. Dan had been a-train-in', Weeks be-fore the

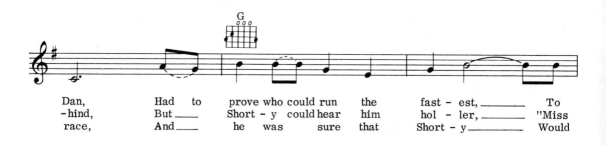

Dan,   Had to prove who could run the fast-est,_____ To
-hind,   But___ Short-y could hear him hol-ler,_____ "Miss
race,   And___ he was sure that Short-y_____ Would

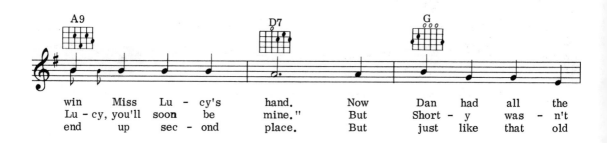

win Miss Lu-cy's hand. Now Dan had all the
Lu-cy, you'll soon be mine." But Short-y was-n't
end up sec-ond place. But just like that old

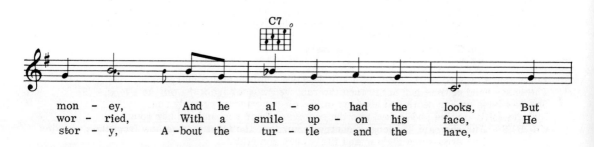

mon-ey, And he al-so had the looks, But
wor-ried, With a smile up-on his face, He
stor-y, A-bout the tur-tle and the hare,

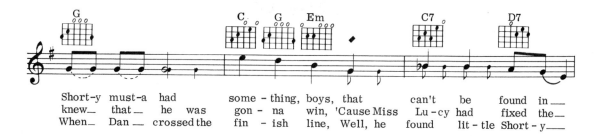

Short-y must-a had   some - thing, boys, that   can't   be   found in ___
knew__ that __ he was   gon - na   win, 'Cause Miss   Lu - cy had   fixed the__
When__ Dan __ crossed the   fin - ish line, Well, he   found   lit - tle Short - y__

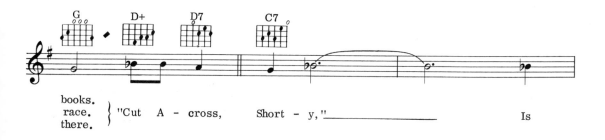

books.
race.   } "Cut A - cross,   Short - y," _____   Is
there.

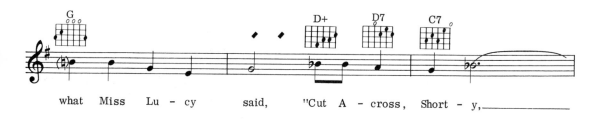

what Miss Lu - cy   said,   "Cut A - cross,   Short - y, _____

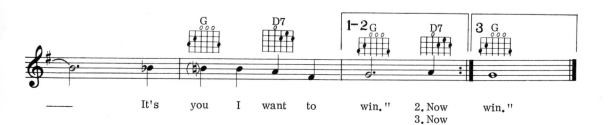

_____ It's   you   I   want   to   win."   2. Now   win."
                                                                    3. Now

SINGER SONG W TAS
M3
COUNTRY 2
BLS 2 ↑80
MB
·COUNTRY SWING BALLAD
0/ 2   1

COOL & BEAT
B

Crazy

Words & Music **Willie Nelson**

Moderately slow

Cra-zy,___ cra-zy for feel-in' so lone-ly.___ I'm

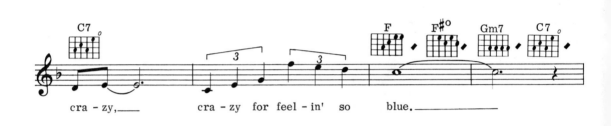

cra-zy,___ cra-zy for feel-in' so blue.___

I knew___ you'd love me as long as you want-ed,___ And then

some-day,___ you'd leave me for some-bod-y new.___

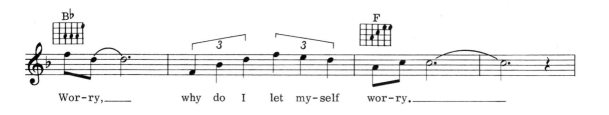

Wor-ry,_____ why do I let my-self wor-ry._____

Won-d'rin',_ what in the world did I do?_____

Cra-zy,_____ for think-ing that my love could hold you,_____ I'm

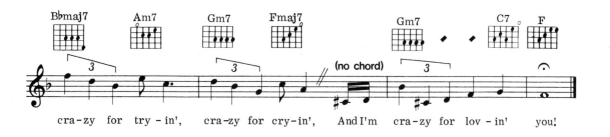

cra-zy for try-in', cra-zy for cry-in', And I'm cra-zy for lov-in' you!

COUNTRY ROCK
M4 TJ35

18
Crazy Arms

Words & Music **Chuck Seals & Ralph Mooney**

Blue is not the word____ for the way____ that I
Please take the trea-sured dreams I've had for you and

feel. And a storm is brew-ing in this heart of
me. And take all the in love I thought was

mine._____ This ain't no
mine._____ Some - day my

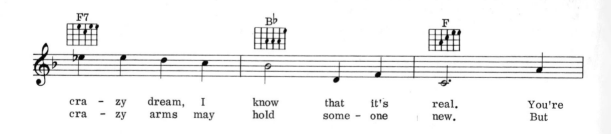

cra - zy dream, I know that it's real. You're
cra - zy arms may hold some - one new. But

some - one else - 's love now you're not mine._____
now I'm so lone - ly all the time._____

Cra - zy Arms that reach to hold some - bod - y

new, But my yearn - ing heart keeps say - ing you're not

mine._____ My trou - bled mind knows

soon to an - oth - er you'll be wed, And

that's why I'm lone - ly all the time._____

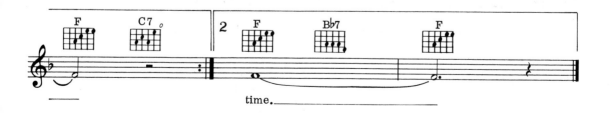

_____ time._____

19
Cryin' Time

Words & Music **Buck Owens**

Moderato

Now they say that ab-sence makes the heart grow fon-der, ___ And that

tears are on - ly rain to make love grow. Well my

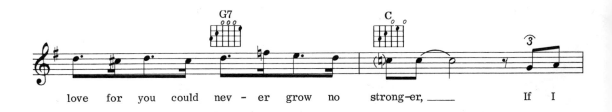

love for you could nev - er grow no strong-er, ___ If I

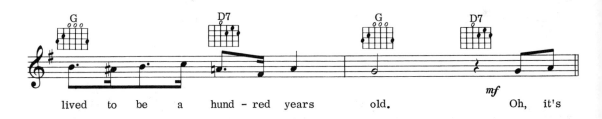

lived to be a hund - red years old. Oh, it's

Chorus

Cry - in' Time a - gain, you're gon - na leave me, ___ I can

see that far a - way look____ in your eyes; I can

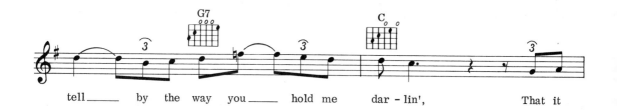

tell____ by the way you____ hold me dar - lin', That it

won't be long be - fore it's_ Cry-in' Time. Now you said that you've_ some-one_ you love

bet - ter.___ That's the way it's hap-pened ev-'ry time be - fore. And as

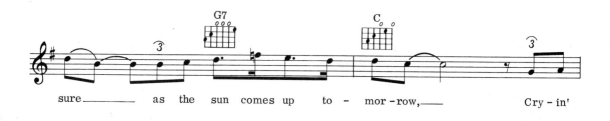

sure_____ as the sun comes up to - mor-row,____ Cry - in'

Time will start when you walk ____ out the door. Oh, it's

Daddy Was An Old Time Preacher Man

Words & Music **Dolly Parton & Dorothy Jo Hope**

Dad-dy was an old time preach-er man;_____ He preached the word of God through-out the land._____ He preached so plain a child could un-der-stand. Yes,_____ Dad-dy was an old time preach-er man._____ *Fine*

1. He told the peo-ple of the need to pray._____ He
2. viv-als and camp meet-ings went for weeks._____ Folks
3. Dad-dy worked for God but asked no pay,_____ For

talked a-bout God's wrath and judge-ment day._____ He
came from all a-round to hear him preach._____ Dad-dy
he be-lieved that God pro-vides a way._____ We

preached a-bout the great e-ter-ni-ty. He preached
said if one is saved it's worth it all. But the
ne-ver had a lot but we got by. Guess it's

21
Daytime Friends

Words & Music **Ben Peters**

22
Deep In The Heart Of Texas

Words **June Hershey**
Music **Don Swander**

Moderately bright

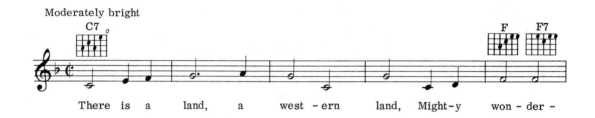

There is a land, a west-ern land, Might-y won-der-

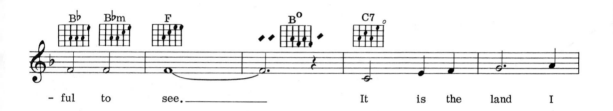

-ful to see. ___ It is the land I

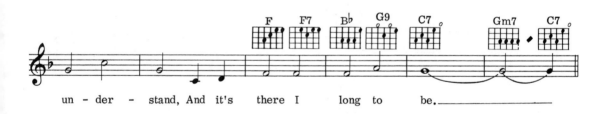

un-der-stand, And it's there I long to be. ___

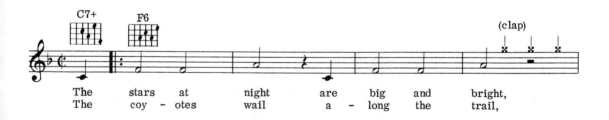

The stars at night are big and bright, (clap)
The coy-otes wail a-long the trail,

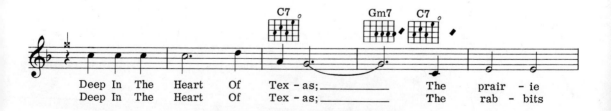

Deep In The Heart Of Tex-as; ___ The prair-ie
Deep In The Heart Of Tex-as; ___ The rab-bits

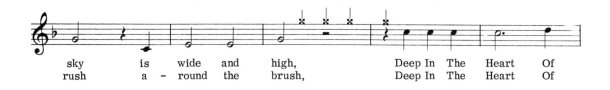

sky is wide and high, Deep In The Heart Of
rush a – round the brush, Deep In The Heart Of

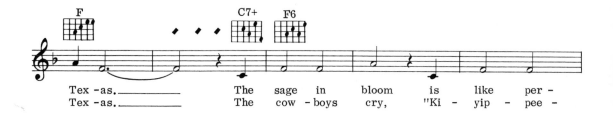

Tex -as._____ The sage in bloom is like per –
Tex -as._____ The cow – boys cry, "Ki – yip – pee –

– fume. Deep In The Heart Of Te – xas;_____ Re –
– vi," Deep In The Heart Of Te – xas;_____ The

– minds me of the one I love, Deep In The
dog – ies bawl, and bawl and bawl, Deep In The

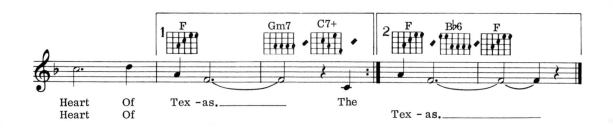

Heart Of Tex -as._____ The
Heart Of   Tex -as._____

Delta Day
(No Time To Cry)

Words & Music **Kris Kristofferson & Marijohn Wilkin**

Moderato

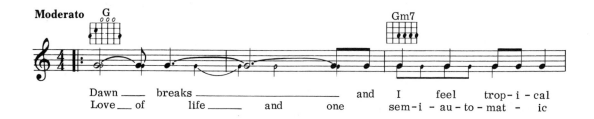

Dawn ___ breaks _____ and I feel trop-i-cal
Love ___ of life ___ and one sem-i-au-to-mat-ic

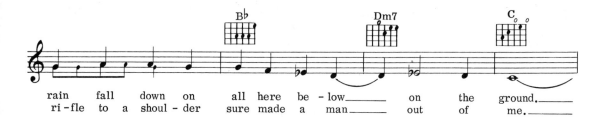

rain fall down on all here be - low _____ on the ground. ___
ri-fle to a shoul - der sure made a man ___ out of me. ___

___ Men walk-ing to hear the sound of
___ Face to face ___ I see the eyes of the

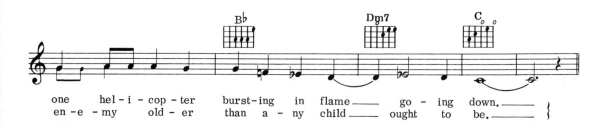

one hel-i-cop-ter burst-ing in flame ___ go - ing down. ___
en-e-my old-er than a - ny child ___ ought to be. ___

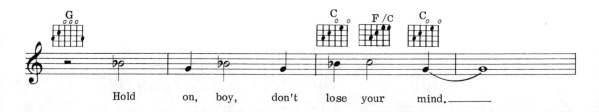

Hold on, boy, don't lose your mind. ___

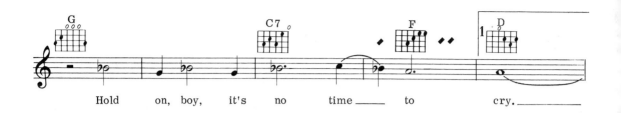

Hold on, boy, it's no time ____ to cry. ____

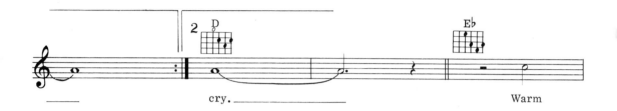

____ cry. ____ Warm

whis-pers, soft ____ sum - mer laugh - ter, "I

love you's" don't fade a - way, old

feel - ings al - most for - got - ten, wait for

me; just one more Del - ta Day. ____

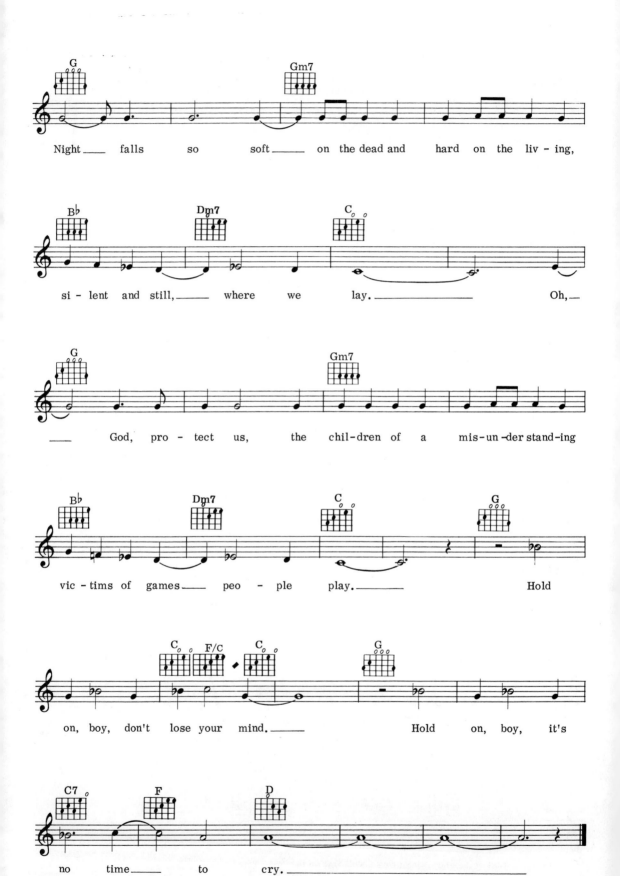

Night ___ falls so soft ___ on the dead and hard on the liv-ing,

si-lent and still, ___ where we lay. ___ Oh, ___

___ God, pro-tect us, the chil-dren of a mis-un-der-stand-ing

vic-tims of games ___ peo-ple play. ___ Hold

on, boy, don't lose your mind. ___ Hold on, boy, it's

no time ___ to cry.

24
Don't Fall In Love With A Dreamer

Words & Music **Kim Carnes & Dave Ellingson**

25
Detroit City

Words & Music Danny Dill & Mel Tillis

Moderato

(1) Last night I went to sleep in De - troit Ci - ty.
(2) Home folks think I'm big in De - troit Ci - ty.

and I dreamed a - bout the cot - ton fields and
from the let - ters that I write they think I'm

home; _____ I dreamed a - bout my
fine; _____ But by day I make the

mo - ther, dear old pa - pa, sis - ter and broth - er, and I
cars, _____ by _____ night I make the bars; _____ if

dreamed a - bout the girl who's been wait - ing for so
on - ly they could

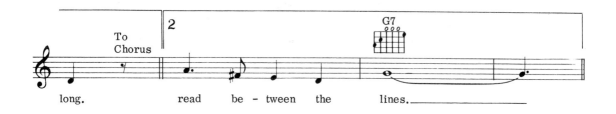

long.   read be - tween the lines._____

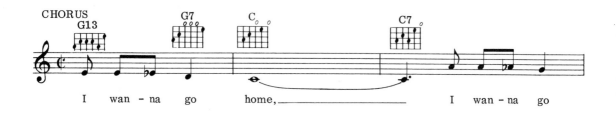

CHORUS

I wan - na go home,_____ I wan - na go

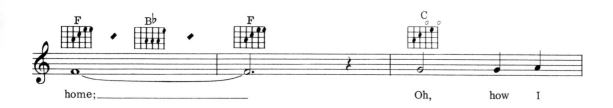

home;_____ Oh, how I

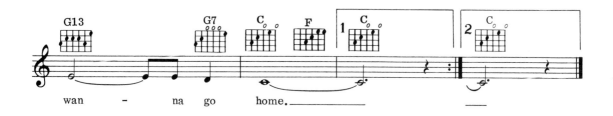

wan - na go home._____   _____

RECITATION

'Cause you know I rode a freight train north to Detroit City,
And after all these years I find I've just been wasting my time.
So I just think I'll take my foolish pride and put it on the
    south-bound freight and ride,
And go on back to the loved ones,
The ones that I left waiting so far behind.   (CHORUS)

26
D.I.V.O.R.C.E.

Words & Music **Bobby Braddock, Curly Putman & Sheb Wooley**

Moderato

Our lit- tle boy is four years old, And quite a lit- tle
Watch him smile, he thinks it's Christ - mas or his fifth birth-

man; So we spell out the words we don't want
day; And he thinks c - u - s - t - o - d -

him to un - der - stand. Like t - o - y or may-be
y spells fun or play. I spell out all the

s - u - r - p - r - i - s - e; But the
hurt- in' words and turn my head when I speak, Be - cause

words we're hid - ing from him now tear the heart right out of
I can't spell a - way this hurt that's drip - pin' down my

27
Don't Get Around Much Anymore

Words **Bob Russell**
Music **Duke Ellington**

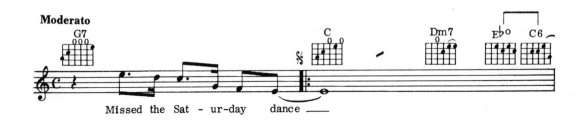

Missed the Sat - ur-day dance ___

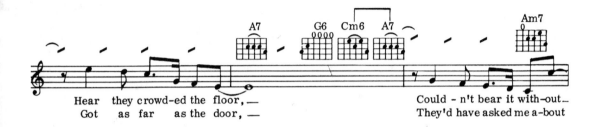

Hear they crowd-ed the floor, ___ Could - n't bear it with-out ___
Got as far as the door, ___ They'd have asked me a-bout

___ you, ___ Don't get a-round much an - y - more.
___ you, ___ Don't get a-round much an - y -

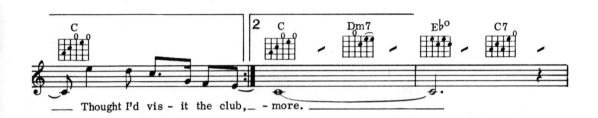

___ Thought I'd vis - it the club, ___ -more. ___

28
Do That To Me One More Time

Words & Music **Toni Tennille**

Moderately with feeling

1.3. Do that to me one more __ time, __ once is nev - er e - nough
2. pac - i - fy me one more __ time, __ once just is - n't e - nough

__ with a man like you. __
__ for my heart to hear. __

Do that to me one more __ time, __ I can nev - er get e -
Tell it to me one more __ time, __ I can nev - er hear e -

- nough of a man like you. __ Oh __
- nough while I got you near. __ Oh __

Kiss __ me __ like you just __ did, __
Say those words a - gain __ like you just __ did, __

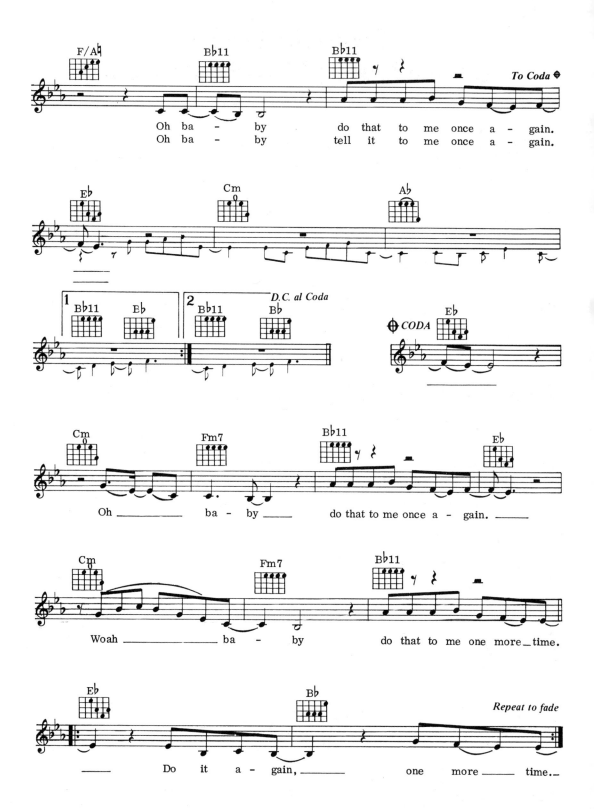

29

Dream Baby
(How Long Must I Dream)

Words & Music **Cindy Walker**

COUNTRY POP 150
M2

BOY BAND
POP PAGE 4

30
Don't It Make My Brown Eyes Blue

Words & Music **Richard Leigh**

1. Don't know when   I've been so blue,___   don't know what's come
2. I'll be fine   when you're gone,___   I'll just cry

o - ver you,   You've found some-one   new ___   and
all night long,___   Say it is - n't   true ___   and

don't it make my brown eyes blue. ___   don't it make my brown eyes blue.

Tell me no se - crets,   tell me some lies,   Give me no rea - sons,—give me

al - i - bies.   Tell me you love me and don't ___ let me cry,___

D. S. al Coda ⊕ *CODA*

Say an-y-thing but don't say good-bye. ___   don't it make my brown eyes,

Repeat to fade

don't it make my brown eyes, don't it make my brown eyes   blue.   And

31
Dreams Of The Everyday Housewife

Words & Music **Chris Gantry**

Moderato

She looks in the mir - ror and stares at the
(The) pho - to - graph al - bum she takes from the

wrink - les that were - n't there yes - ter - day.____
clos - et and slow - ly turns the first page;____

and thinks of the young man that she al - most
And care - ful - ly picks up the crum - bl - ing

Mar - ried;____ What would he think if he saw her this
flow - er; The first one he gave her, now with - ered with

way?_____ She holds up her a - pron in
age;_____ She clos - es her eyes and

lit - tle girl fash - ion, as some - thing comes in - to her
touch - es the house - dress that sud - den - ly dis - ap -

32

Driving My Life Away

Words & Music **Eddie Rabbit, Even Stevens & David Malloy**

1.3. Well, the mid - night head - lights
2 (see additional lyrics)

blind you on a rain - y night; steep grade up a - head,

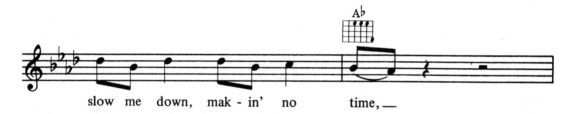

slow me down, mak - in' no time, ___

but I got to keep ___ roll -

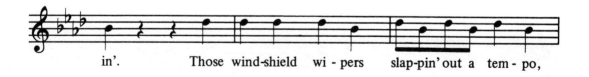

in'. Those wind-shield wi - pers slap-pin' out a tem - po,

keep -in' per-fect rhy -thm with the song ___ on the ra - di - o, ___

but I got to keep— roll - in'.

CHORUS

Ooh, _____ I'm driv - in' my life a - way,

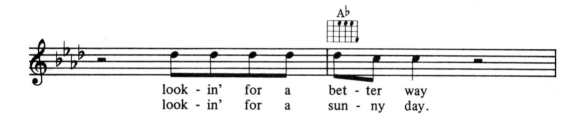

look - in' for a bet - ter way
look - in' for a sun - ny day.

1. for _____ me.
2. & fade last time

D. % (Twice)

Well, the

2. Well, the truck stop cutie comin' on to me,
    Tried to talk me into a ride;
    Said I wouldn't be sorry, but she was just a baby.
    Hey, waitress, pour me another cup of coffee,
    Pop it down, jack me up, shoot me out, flyin' down the highway,
    Lookin' for the mornin'. (To Chorus:)

33
Every Now And Then

Words & Music **Shayne Dolan & Rock Killough**

When we
need - ed help the most, we found each oth - er, _____
2. made each oth - er laugh, like hap - py chil - dren,

_____ and with - out you, I don't know where I'd have been; _____
you have some - times felt my tear - drops on your hand; _____

We have soothed each oth - er's qui - et des - per - a -
And _____ when we can't con - trol our lone - ly feel -

- tion, _____ And loved each oth - er ev - 'ry now and
- ings, _____ We loved each oth - er ev - 'ry now and

1. (Instr.)

2.3.

then.   2. We have then. _____   We're a

CHORUS

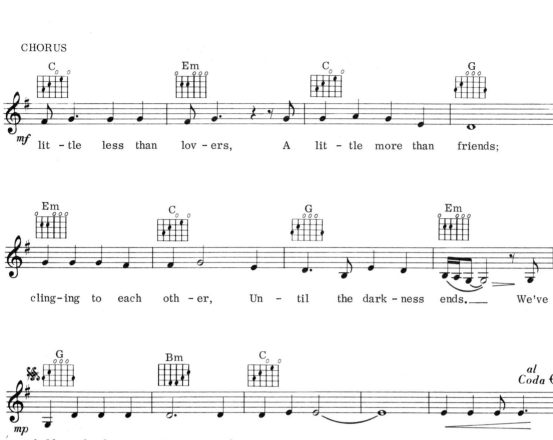

lit - tle less than lov - ers, A lit - tle more than friends;

cling-ing to each oth - er, Un - til the dark - ness ends.____ We've

held each oth - er time and time a - gain;_____ loved each oth - er

ev - 'ry now and then. _____ then. _____

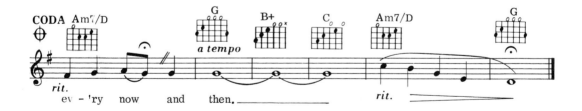

ev - 'ry now and then. _____

(Verse 3)   Someday I'll find the one who's meant for me,
            And I know that someday you'll find love again;
            But we'll always have a very special memory,
            Of the love we gave each other now and then.

34
Everybody's Talkin'

Words & Music **Fred Neil**

Ev-'ry-bod-y's talk-in' at __ me, I don't hear a word they're say-in', on -ly the ech-oes __ of my mind. Peo -ple stop-pin', star - in', I can't see their fac - es, on-ly the sha-dows __ of their eyes. I'm go-in' where the sun keeps shin-in', thru' the pour-ing rain. __ Go-in' where the wea-ther suits my cloth - - es, Bank-ing off of the North __ East wind, __ Sail-in' on sum-mer breeze and skip-pin' o-ver the o - cean __ like a stone. __ And I won't let __ you leave __ my love be - hind, __ No

al Coda

D. C. al Coda

⊕ *CODA*

Repeat and Fade

Everything Is Beautiful

Words & Music **Ray Stevens**

Everything Is Beautiful

Words & Music **Ray Stevens**

Forty Shades Of Green

Words & Music **Johnny Cash**

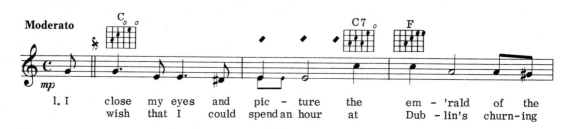

1. I close my eyes and pic - ture the em - 'rald of the
   wish that I could spend an hour at Dub - lin's churn - ing

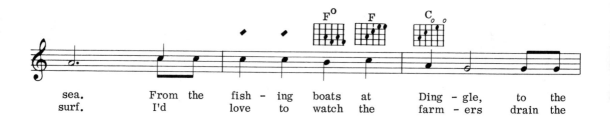

sea. From the fish - ing boats at Ding - gle, to the
surf. I'd love to watch the farm - ers drain the

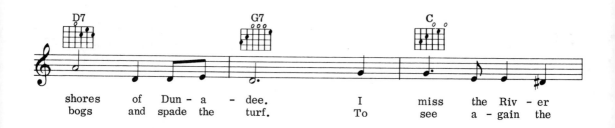

shores of Dun - a - dee. I miss the Riv - er
bogs and spade the turf. To see a - gain the

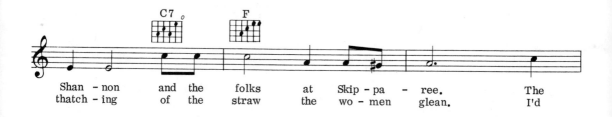

Shan - non and the folks at Skip - pa - ree. The
thatch - ing of the straw the wo - men glean. I'd

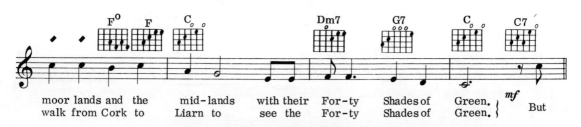

moor lands and the mid - lands with their For - ty Shades of Green. But
walk from Cork to Liarn to see the For - ty Shades of Green.

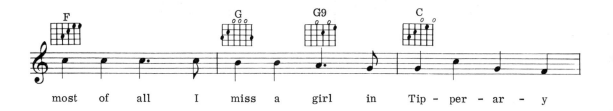

most of all I miss a girl in Tip - per - ar - y

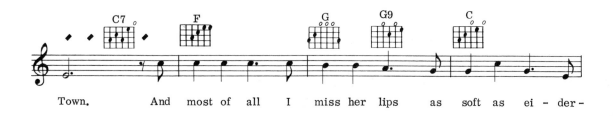

Town. And most of all I miss her lips as soft as ei - der -

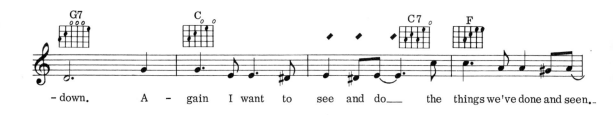

- down. A - gain I want to see and do___ the things we've done and seen.___

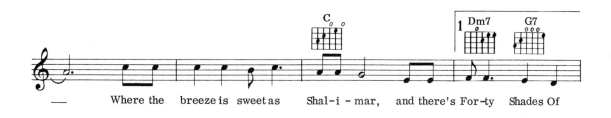

___ Where the breeze is sweet as Shal-i - mar, and there's For-ty Shades Of

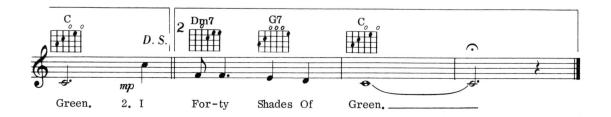

Green. 2. I For-ty Shades Of Green._____

37
Frankie And Johnny

Traditional

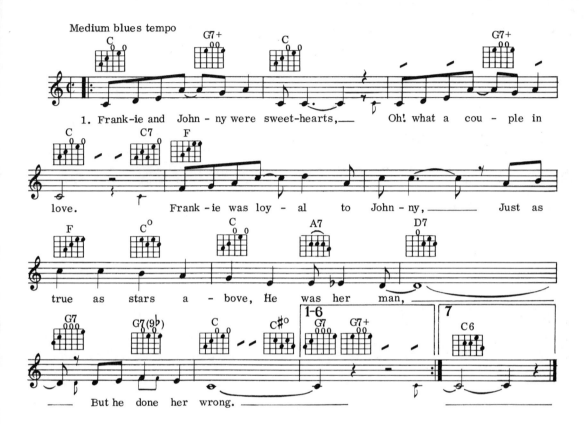

1. Frank-ie and John-ny were sweet-hearts,___ Oh! what a cou-ple in love. Frank-ie was loy-al to John-ny,_____ Just as true as stars a-bove, He was her man,_____ But he done her wrong.___

2. Frankie went down to the drug-store,
Some ice-cream she wanted to buy,
The soda jerk told her that Johnny
Was makin' love to Nellie Bly,
He was her man,
But he was doin' her wrong.

3. Frankie's dad was a police-man,
She stole his old forty-four gun,
Then back to the drug-store she beat it,
Just as fast as she could run,
After her man,
Who was doin' her wrong.

4. Frankie peeked in on the party,
She got a surprise when she saw
That Nellie and Johnny were makin' love
And sippin' soda thru a straw,
He was her man,
But he was doin' her wrong.

5. Frankie flew into a tantrum,
She whipped out that old forty-four,
And her root-ta-ti-toot that gal did shoot
Right thru that hard-wood swingin' door,
She shot her man,
'Cause he was doin' her wrong.

6. Bring on your crepe and your flowers,
And bring on your rubber tyred hack,
'Cause there's eight men to go to the grave-yard,
But only seven are comin' back,
She shot her man,
'Cause he was doin' her wrong.

7. This is the end of my story,
And this is the end of my song,
Frankie is down in the jail-house,
And she cries the whole night long,
"He was my man,
But he done me wrong."

Funny How Time Slips Away

Words & Music **Willie Nelson**

Girl Of My Best Friend

Words & Music **Beverly Ross & Sam Bobrick**

The — way — she — walks, ___ The — way — she — talks, ___
Her — love-ly — hair, ___ Her — skin — so — fair, ___

How_long_can__ I ___ pre - tend. ___ Oh I can't
I _ could_go __ on 'n nev-er end. ___ Oh I can't

help it I'm in love ___ with the girl of my best
help it I'm in love ___ with the girl of my best

1 friend. ___ **2** friend. ___ I want to

tell her how I love her ___ so, And hold her

in my arms, but then ___ What if she

40
Good Year For The Roses

Words & Music **Jerry Chesnut**

I can hard-ly bear the sight of lip-stick on the cigarettes there in the
three full years of mar-riage, it's the first time that you have-n't made the

ash - tray, ly-ing cold the way you left 'em, but at
bed. I guess the reas-on we're not talk-ing, there's so

least **your** lips car-ressed 'em while you packed. And a
lit-tle left to say we have-n't said. While a

lip - print on a half-filled cup of cof-fee that you poured and did-n't
mil - lion thoughts go rac-ing through my mind I find I have-n't said a

drink. But at least you thought you want-ed it, that's
word. From the bed-room the fam-il-iar sound of

CHORUS

so much more than I can say for me. What a good year for the
our one ba - by's cry-ing goes un - heard.

41

Good Ol' Boys
(Dukes Of Hazzard – Theme)

Words & Music **Waylon Jennings**

Verse 2:
Straight'nin' the curve, flat'nin' the hills.
Someday the mountains might get 'em,
But the law never will. (To Chorus)

Verses 3 & 4: Instrumental solos

Verse 5:
I'm a good ol' boy,
You know, my momma loves me,
But she don't understand,
They keep a'showin' my hands,
And no my face on T.V. Hah, hah.

42
Green, Green Grass Of Home

Words & Music **Curly Putman**

The old home town_ looks the same As I step down_ from the train, _____ And there to meet me is my ma-ma_ and pa-pa; _____

old house is still stand-ing, Tho' the paint is cracked and dry, _____ And there's that old oak tree that I used_ to play on; _____

Down the road I look, and there runs Ma-ry,

Down the lane I walk with my sweet Ma-ry, Hair of gold and

lips like cher-ries; It's good to touch the green, green grass of home.

Chorus
1 & 2. Yes, they'll
3. Yes, they'll

all come to meet me, Arms_ reach-ing, smil-ing sweet-ly; It's

all come to see me In the

good to touch the green, green grass of home. 2. The shade of that

old oak tree As they lay me 'neath the green, green grass of home. _____

3. (spoken) Then I awake and look around me at the four grey walls that surround me,
And I realize that I was only dreaming,
For there's a guard and there's a sad old padre - arm in arm we'll walk at daybreak;
Again I'll touch the green, green grass of home. (CHORUS)

43
Heartaches By The Number

Words & Music **Harlan Howard**

Heart-ache num - ber one was when you left me.
Heart-ache num - ber three was when you called me.

I nev - er knew that I could hurt this way.
And said that you were com - ing back to stay.

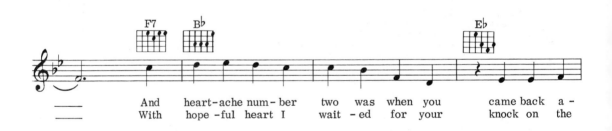

And heart-ache num - ber two was when you came back a -
With hope -ful heart I wait - ed for your knock on the

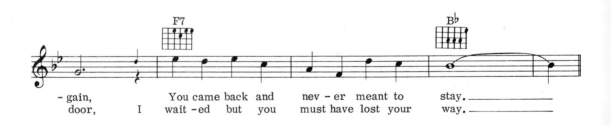

- gain, You came back and nev - er meant to stay.
door, I wait -ed but you must have lost your way.

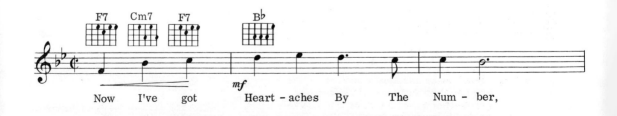

Now I've got Heart - aches By The Num - ber,

Troub - les by the score.   Ev - 'ry day you

love me less, Each day I love you more.

Yes, I've got Heart - aches By The Num - ber, ___ A

love that I can't win, But the day that I stop

1

count - ing, That's the day my world will end. _____

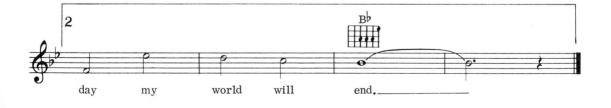

2

day my world will end. _____

44
He'll Have To Go

Words & Music **Joe Allison & Audrey Allison**

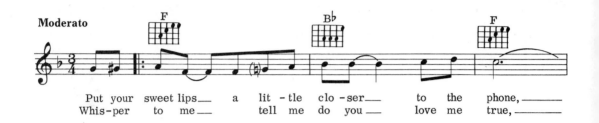

Put your sweet lips a lit-tle clo-ser to the phone,
Whis-per to me tell me do you love me true,

Let's pre-tend that we're to-geth-er, all a-lone.
Or is he hold-ing you the way I do?

I'll tell the man to turn the juke-box way down low,
Tho' love is blind, make up your mind, I've got to know,

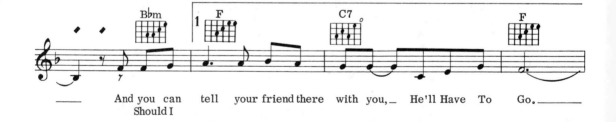

And you can tell your friend there with you, He'll Have To Go.
Should I

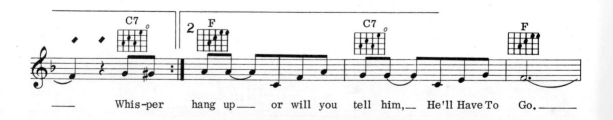

Whis-per hang up or will you tell him, He'll Have To Go.

You can't say the words I want to hear, while you're with an -oth -er

man, If you want me, an-swer "Yes" or "No" Dar -ling, I will un -der -

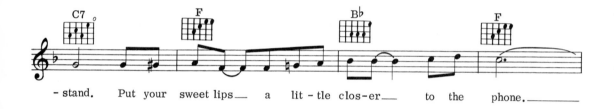

- stand. Put your sweet lips__ a lit -tle clos-er__ to the phone._____

_____ Let's pre - tend that we're to - geth - er, all a - lone._____

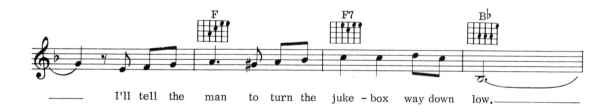

_____ I'll tell the man to turn the juke - box way down low._____

_____ And you can tell your friend there with you, __ He'll Have To Go._____

COUNTRY BLUES MC

45
Hello Walls
Words & Music Willie Nelson

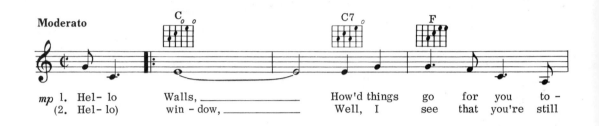

Moderato

mp 1. Hel- lo   Walls, _____   How'd things   go   for   you   to-
(2. Hel- lo)   win - dow, _____   Well, I   see   that   you're   still

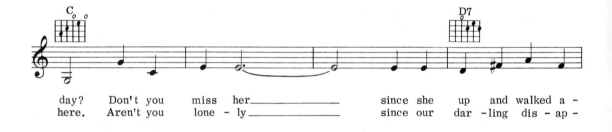

day?   Don't you   miss   her_____   since   she   up   and   walked a -
here.   Aren't you   lone - ly_____   since   our   dar -ling   dis - ap -

way?   And I'll   bet   you   dread to   spend an - oth - er   lone - ly   night with
peared?   Well, look   here,   is   that a   tear-drop   in   the   cor - ner of   your

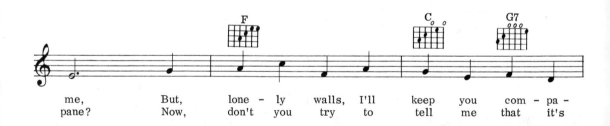

me,   But,   lone - ly   walls, I'll   keep   you   com - pa -
pane?   Now,   don't   you   try   to   tell   me   that   it's

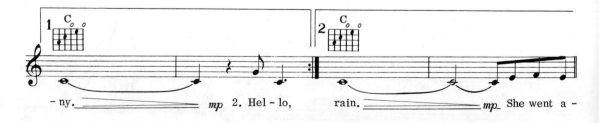

1. - ny. _____   mp 2. Hel - lo,   rain. _____   mp 2. - She went a -
rain. _____

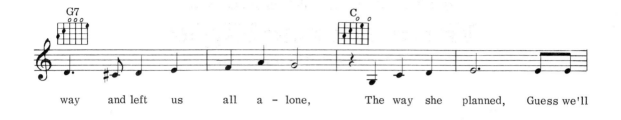

way and left us all a - lone, The way she planned, Guess we'll

have to learn to get a - long with - out her if we can; Hel - lo

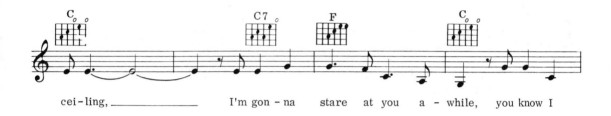

cei - ling, _____ I'm gon - na stare at you a - while, you know I

can't sleep, _____ so won't you bear with me a - while? We must

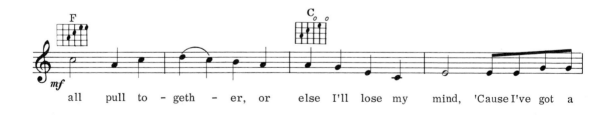

all pull to - geth - er, or else I'll lose my mind, 'Cause I've got a

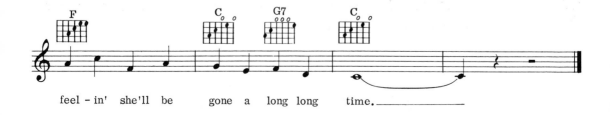

feel - in' she'll be gone a long long time. _____

46
Help Me Make It Through The Night

Words & Music **Kris Kristofferson**

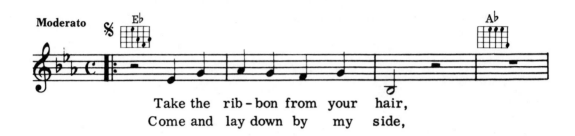

Take the rib-bon from your hair,
Come and lay down by my side,

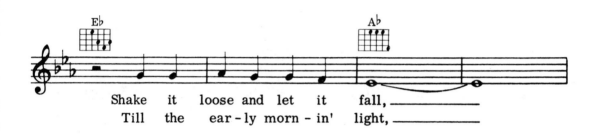

Shake it loose and let it fall, _____
Till the ear-ly morn-in' light, _____

Lay-in' soft up-on my skin, _____
All I'm tak-in' is your time, _____

Like the shad-ows on the wall,

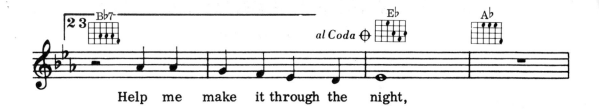

Help me make it through the night,

I don't care who's right or wrong;

I don't try to un - der - stand;

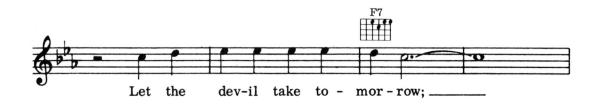

Let the dev-il take to - mor - row;

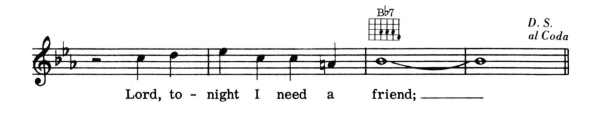

Lord, to - night I need a friend;

CODA

night.

47

Here I Am Drunk Again

Words & Music **Jack Kay & Autry Inman**

Easy Country two-beat

Am, I'm Drunk A - gain; _____ I'm drunk be-

- cause you are gone. _____ At the bar I'm

stand - ing all a - lone. _____ drown - ing my

sor - row deep with - in; _____ Here I

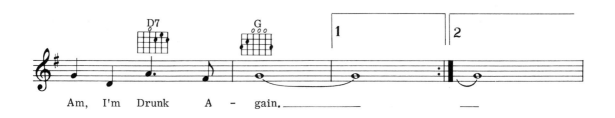

Am, I'm Drunk A - gain. _____

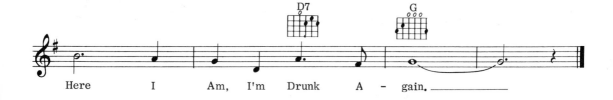

Here I Am, I'm Drunk A - gain. _____

48
He Stopped Loving Her Today

Words & Music **Bobby Braddock & Curly Putman**

Very slow ♩ = 72

1. He said "I'll love you 'til I die." She told him "You'll forget in
2. wall; went half cra - zy now and
3.4.5. (see additional lyrics)

time." As the years went slow - ly by,
then, but he still loved her through it all,

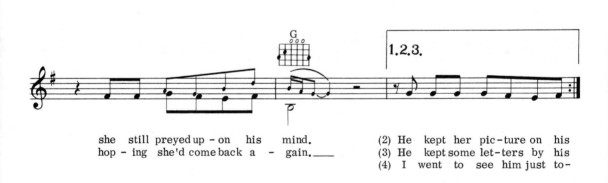

she still preyed up - on his mind. (2) He kept her pic - ture on his
hop - ing she'd come back a - gain.___ (3) He kept some let - ters by his
(4) I went to see him just to-

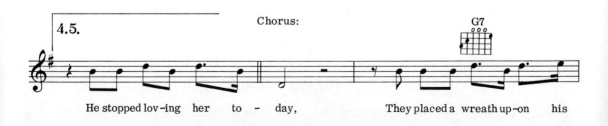

4.5. **Chorus:**

He stopped lov - ing her to - day, They placed a wreath up - on his

door,___   and soon they'll car - ry him a - way.___

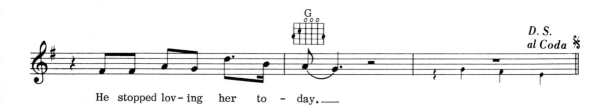

He stopped lov - ing her to - day.___

CODA

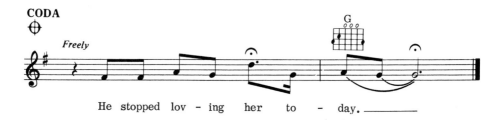

Freely

He stopped lov - ing her to - day._____

Verse 3:   He kept some letters by his bed, dated 1962,
                He had underlined in red every single "I love you."

Verse 4:   I went to see him just today, oh, but I didn't see no tears;
                All dressed up to go away, first time I'd seen him smile in years.
                (To Chorus)

Verse 5:   You know, she came to see him one last time,
(Spoken:) We all wondered if she would.
                And it came running through my mind,
                This time he's over her for good.
                (To Chorus)

49
Husbands And Wives

Words & Music **Roger Miller**

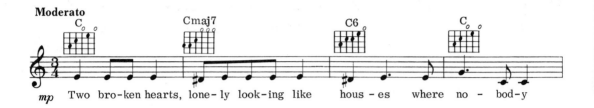

Two bro-ken hearts, lone-ly look-ing like hous—es where no-bod-y

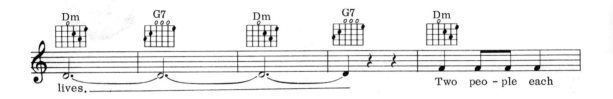

lives._____ Two peo-ple each

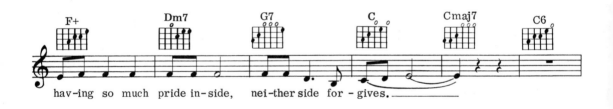

hav-ing so much pride in-side, nei-ther side for-gives._____

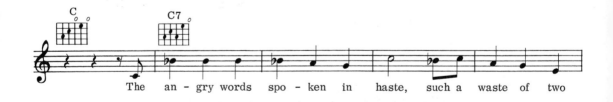

The an-gry words spo-ken in haste, such a waste of two

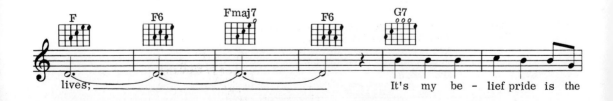

lives;_____ It's my be-lief pride is the

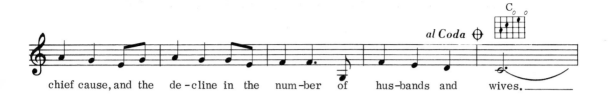

chief cause, and the de-cline in the num-ber of hus-bands and wives. _____

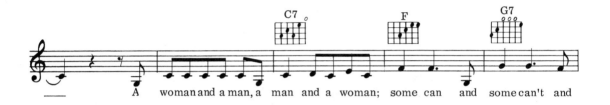

_____ A woman and a man, a man and a woman; some can and some can't and

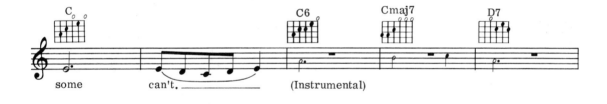

some can't. _____ (Instrumental)

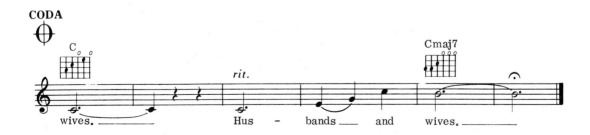

CODA

wives. _____ Hus - bands _____ and wives. _____

50

I Can't Stop Loving You

Words & Music **Billy Nicholls**

So you're leav - ing in the
We took a tax - i to the

morn - ing on the ear - ly train.
sta - tion not a word was said,

I could say ev - 'ry-thing's al-
I saw you walk a - cross the

- right.
road, For may - be the last time but I don't

-bye.
know. I'm feel-ing hum - ble, I heard a

suit - case, got your leav - ing smile,
rum - ble on the rail - way track,

I could pre - tend and say good-

Got your tick - et, got your

51
I'd Rather Be Sorry

Words & Music **Kris Kristofferson**

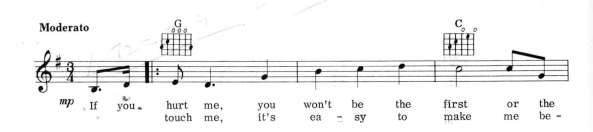

If you hurt me, you won't be the first or the
touch me, it's ea-sy to make me be-

last in a life-time of man-y mis-
lieve to-mor-row won't take you a-

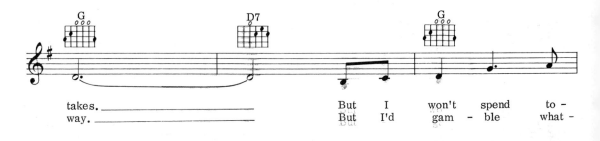

takes._____ But I won't spend to-
way._____ But I'd gam-ble what-

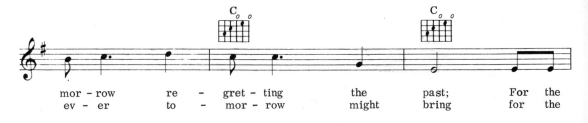

mor-row re-gret-ting the past; For the
ev-er to-mor-row might bring for the

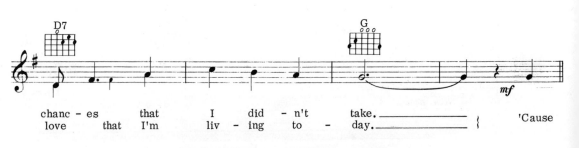

chanc-es that I did-n't take._____ 'Cause
love that I'm liv-ing to-day._____ {

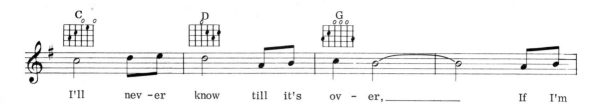

I'll   nev -er   know   till   it's   ov - er,_____   If   I'm

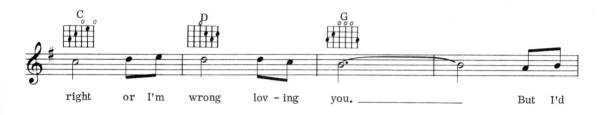

right   or   I'm   wrong   lov - ing   you. _____   But   I'd

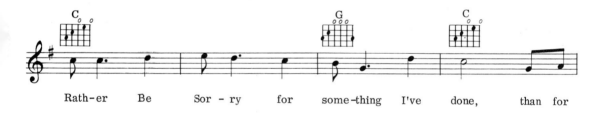

Rath- er   Be   Sor - ry   for   some -thing   I've   done,   than   for

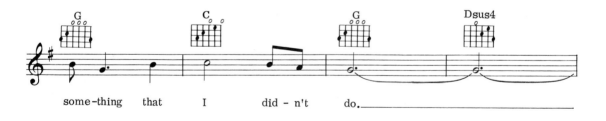

some -thing   that   I   did - n't   do._____

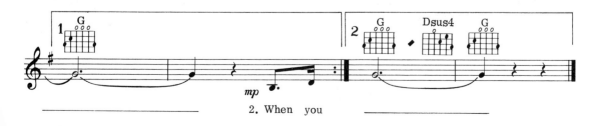

mp
_____   2. When   you   _____

52
Guess Things Happen That Way

Words & Music **Jack Clement**

1. You ask me if I'll for-get my ba-by. I guess I will
(2. You) ask me if I'll___ miss her kiss-es. I guess I will

some___ day. I don't like it but I guess things hap-pen that way.
ev-'ry day. I don't like it but I guess things hap-pen that way.

You ask me if I'll get a -long.___ I guess I will
You ask me if I'll find an -oth-er. I don't___ know;

some way. } I don't like it but I guess things hap-pen that way.___
I can't say. }

God gave me that girl to lean on; Then He put me on my own.___

Heav-en help me be a man and have the strength to stand a-lone.___

I don't like it but I guess things hap-pen that way.___ 2. You ___

53
I Fall To Pieces

Words & Music **Hank Cochran & Harlan Howard**

Moderato

I Fall____ To Piec - es,____
I Fall____ To Piec - es,____

each time I see you a - gain.____ I
each time some - one speaks your name.____ I

Fall____ To Piec - es,____ How can I be just your
Fall____ To Piec - es,____ Time on-ly adds to the

friend?____ You want me to act like we've nev - er kissed,—
flame.____ You tell me to find some - one else to love,—

You want me to for - get, pre-tend we've nev - er met,____ And I've
Some - one who'll love me too the way you used to do,____ But each

tried____ and I've tried, but I have - n't yet,____ You walk by and
time____ I go out with____ some-one new,____ You walk by and

1
I Fall To Piec - es.____

2
Piec - es.____

54
I Love A Rainy Night

Words & Music **Eddie Rabbit, Even Stevens & David Malloy**

Well I Love _____ A Rain - y Night, I Love A Rain - y Night, I

love to hear the thun - der, watch the light-ning when it lights up the sky.__

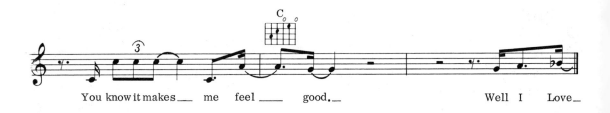

You know it makes __ me feel __ good. __ Well I Love __

__ A Rain- y Night, It's such a beau-ti-ful sight,_ I love to feel the rain_on my face,

__ Taste the rain on my lips._____ In the moon - light

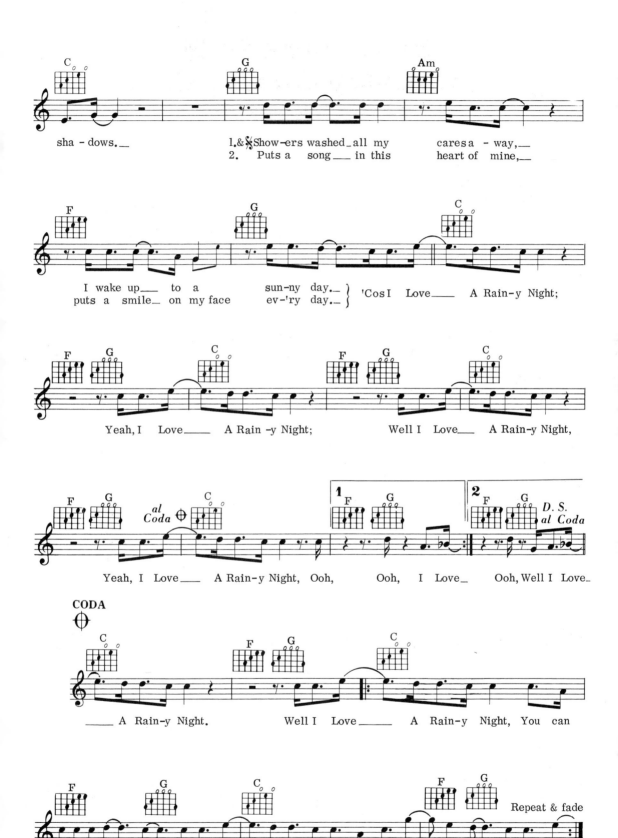

55

I'm Gonna Be A Country Girl Again

Words & Music **Buffy Sainte Marie**

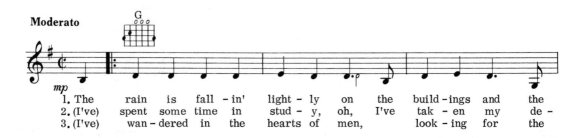

1. The rain is fall-in' light-ly on the build-ings and the
2. (I've) spent some time in stud-y, oh, I've tak-en my de-
3. (I've) wan-dered in the hearts of men, look-ing for the

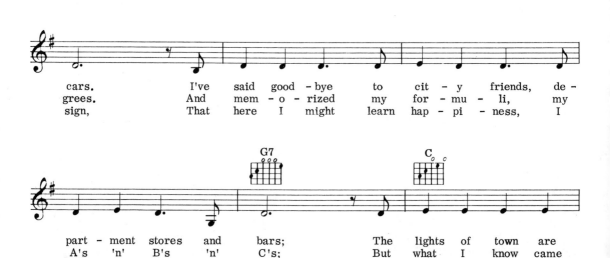

cars. I've said good-bye to cit-y friends, de-
grees. And mem-o-rized my for-mu-li, my
sign, That here I might learn hap-pi-ness, I

part-ment stores and bars; The lights of town are
A's 'n' B's 'n' C's; But what I know came
might learn peace of mind; The one who taught my

at my back, my heart is full of stars.
long a-go and not from such as these.
les-son was the south wind through the pines.

And I'm

CHORUS

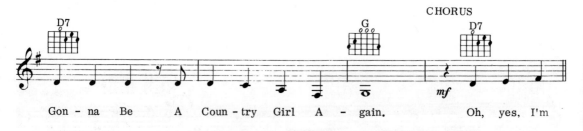

Gon-na Be A Coun-try Girl A-gain.   Oh, yes, I'm

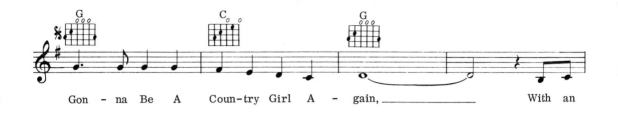

Gon - na Be A Coun-try Girl A - gain, _____ With an

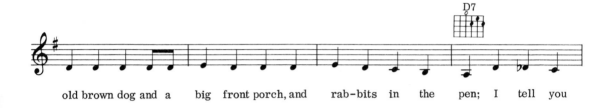

old brown dog and a big front porch, and rab-bits in the pen; I tell you

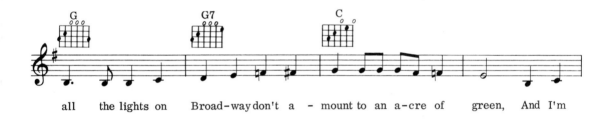

all the lights on Broad-way don't a - mount to an a-cre of green, And I'm

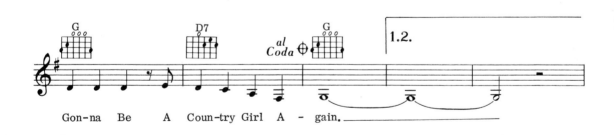

al Coda 1.2.

Gon-na Be A Coun-try Girl A - gain. _____

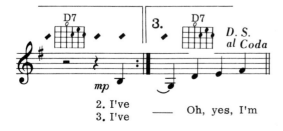

3. *D. S. al Coda*

mp

2. I've
3. I've ——— Oh, yes, I'm

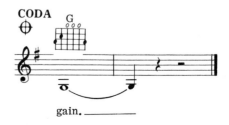

CODA

gain. _____

56
It's Hard To Be Humble

Words & Music **Mac Davis**

Moderato

Oh Lord, It's Hard___ To Be Hum-ble, when you're
per-fect in ev-er-y way___ I can't wait to
look in___ the mir-ror, 'cos I get bet-ter look-in'__ each_ day.__
_____ To__ know me is to love me, I___
must be a hell of a man.___ Oh,__ Lord, It's Hard_
___ To Be Hum-ble,___ But I'm do-in' the best that_ I__

(Instrumental)

can._____

57
It's Not Unusual

Words & Music **Gordon Mills & Les Reed**

Moderately, with a beat

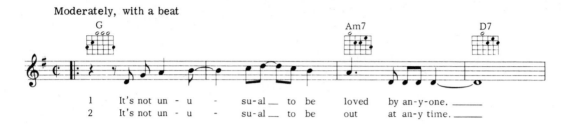

1 It's not un-u-su-al__ to be loved by an-y-one. ____
2 It's not un-u-su-al__ to be out at an-y time. ____

It's not un-u-su-al__ to have fun with an-y-one. ____
But when I see __ you out __ and a-bout, it's such a crime. ____

But when I see __ you hang-ing a-bout __ with an-y-one, ____
If you should ev-er wan-na be loved__ by an-y-one, ____

It's not un-u-su-al__ to see me cry. ____ I wan-na die. ____
It's not un-u-su-al,__ it

hap-pens ev'-ry day. ____ No mat-ter what__ you say,

EASY COUNTR ? ML

58
Lonesome Road

Words & Music **Gene Austin & Nathaniel Shilkret**

mf Look down, look down, that lone - some road, __ Be -

fore you trav - el on. _____ Look up, look up, and

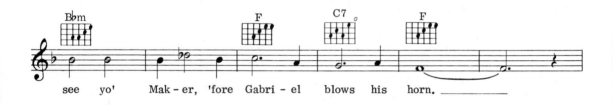

see yo' Mak - er, 'fore Gabri - el blows his horn. _____

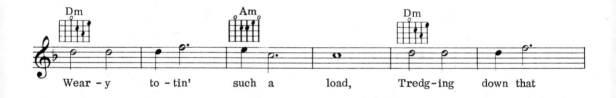

Wear - y to - tin' such a load, Tredg - ing down that

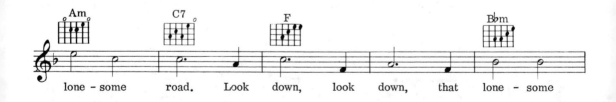

lone - some road. Look down, look down, that lone - some

road, __ Be - fore you trav - el on. _____ Look __

COPY →

It Was Almost Like A Song

Words & Music **Hal David & Archie Jordan**

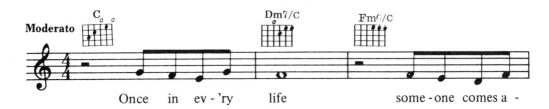

Once in ev-'ry life some-one comes a-

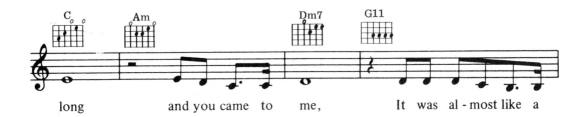

long and you came to me, It was al-most like a

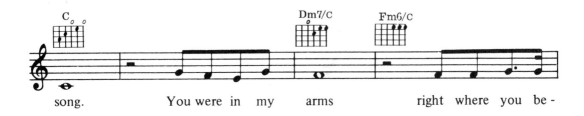

song. You were in my arms right where you be-

long and we were so in love___

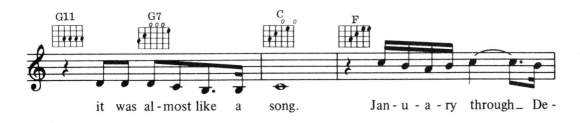

it was al-most like a song. Jan-u-a-ry through_ De-

cem - ber   we had such a per - fect   year

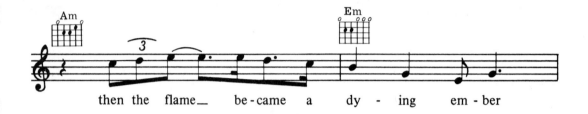

then the flame___ be - came a dy - ing em - ber

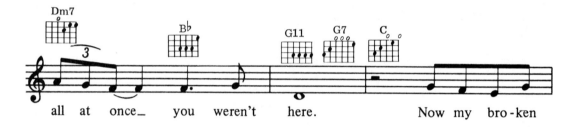

all at once___ you weren't here.   Now my bro - ken

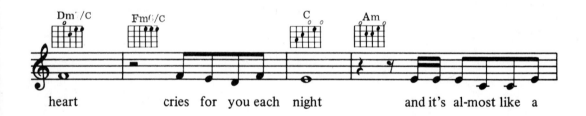

heart   cries for you each night   and it's al-most like a

song_____   but it's much too sad to write.

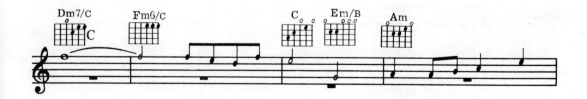

59
It Was Almost Like A Song

Words & Music **Hal David & Archie Jordan**

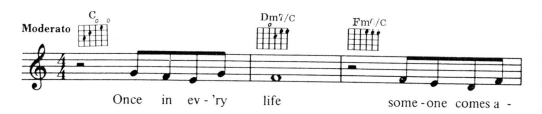

Once in ev-'ry life some-one comes a-

long and you came to me, It was al-most like a

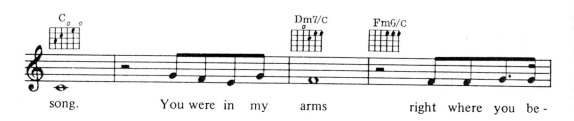

song. You were in my arms right where you be-

long and we were so in love____

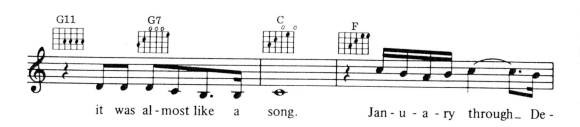

it was al-most like a song. Jan-u-a-ry through_ De-

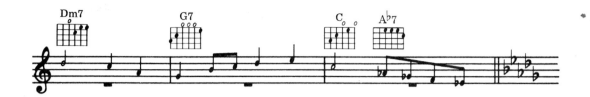

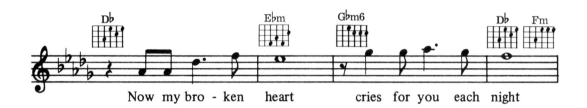

Now my bro - ken   heart   cries for you   each night

and it's al - most like   a   song

—   but it's much too sad to   write._____   It's too sad to

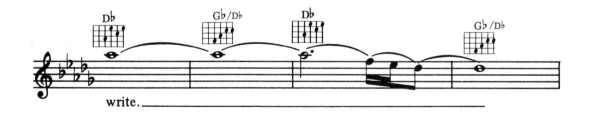

write._____

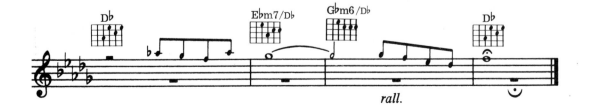

rall.

60
I've Always Been Crazy

Words & Music **Waylon Jennings**

Moderato

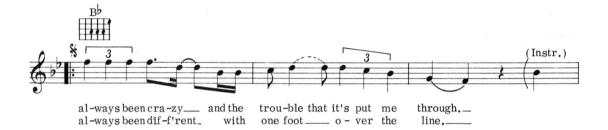

al-ways been cra-zy__ and the trou-ble that it's put me through.__
al-ways been dif-f'rent__ with one foot__ o-ver the line.__

And bust-ed__ for things that I did and I did-n't
wind-in'__ up some-where one step a-head or be-

do. I can't say I'm proud of all of the things that I've
hind. It ain't been so eas-y, I guess I should-n't com-

done. But I can say I nev-er in-
plain. I've__ al-ways been cra-zy, it's

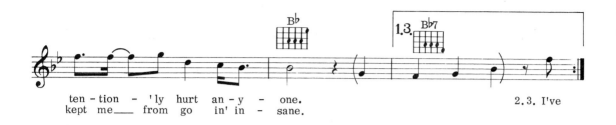

ten - tion - 'ly hurt an - y - one.
kept me____ from go in' in - sane.

2.3. I've

Beau - ti - ful la - dy, are you sure that you un - der -
you real - ly sure, you real - ly want what you

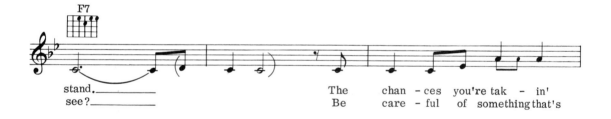

stand._____ The chan - ces you're tak - in'
see?_____ Be care - ful of something that's

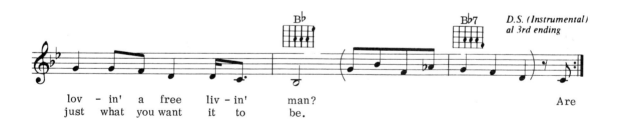

lov - in' a free liv - in' man? Are
just what you want it to be.

3. I've always been crazy, but it's kept me from goin' insane,
   Nobody knows if it's something to bless or to blame.
   So far I ain't found a rhyme or a reason to change,
   I've always been crazy, but it's kept me from goin' insane.

61

Jackson

Words & Music **Billy Edd Wheeler & Gaby Rogers**

1. We got mar - ried in a fev - er, Hot-ter than a pep-per
3. I breeze in to that cit - y, Peo-ple gon - na stoop and

sprout. We've been talk - in' 'bout Jack - son,
bow. All them wo - men goin' beg me,

ev - er since the fire went out. I'm goin' to Jack - son,
teach 'em what they don't know how. I'm goin' to Jack - son,

I'm gon-na mess a - round, Yeah, I'm goin' to Jack-son,
You turn a - loose my coat, 'Cause I'm goin' to Jack-son,

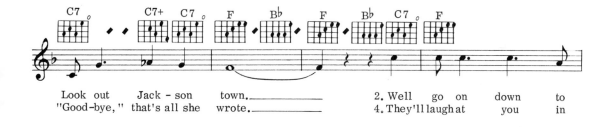

Look out Jack - son town._____ 2. Well go on down to
"Good-bye," that's all she wrote._____ 4. They'll laugh at you in

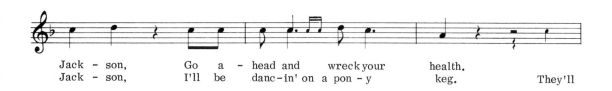

Jack - son, Go a - head and wreck your health.
Jack - son, I'll be danc-in' on a pon - y keg. They'll

Go play your hand, ya big talk - in' man, make a big fool of your - self,_
lead you 'round town, a scold-ed hound, with your tail tucked 'tween your legs,_

_____ yeah yeah, go to Jack-son, But go comb your hair.__
_____ yeah yeah, go to Jack-son, You big talk-in' man.__

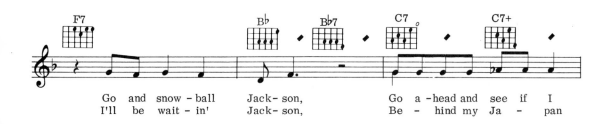

Go and snow - ball Jack- son, Go a -head and see if I
I'll be wait - in' Jack- son, Be - hind my Ja - pan

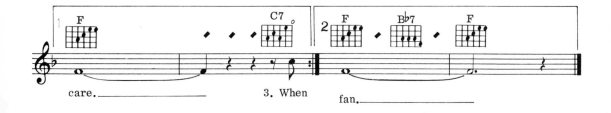

care._____ 3. When
fan._____

62

Jolene

Words & Music **Dolly Parton**

Jo - lene, Jo - lene, Jo - lene, Jo -

-lene, _____   I'm beg - ging of you, please don't take my
please don't take him just be - cause ___ you

man. _____   Jo-
can. _____   Your

beau - ty is be - yond com - pare, with flam - ing locks of
smile is like a breath of spring, your voice is soft like

au - burn hair, with iv - 'ry skin and eyes of em - 'rald
sum - mer rain, ___ and I can - not com - pete with you,

green. _____   Your

Jo - lene. _____   He

63
Lucille

Words & Music **Roger Bowling & Hal Bynum**

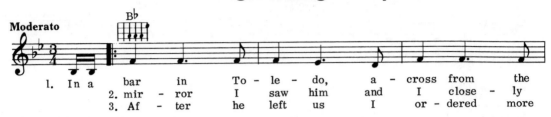

1. In a bar in To-le-do, a - cross from the
2. mir - ror I saw him and I close - ly
3. Af - ter he left us I or - dered more

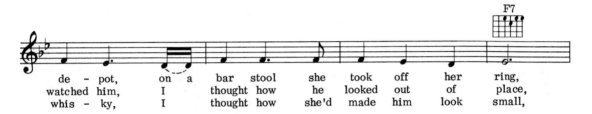

de - pot, on a bar stool she took off her ring,
watched him, I thought how he looked out of place,
whis - ky, I thought how she'd made him look small,

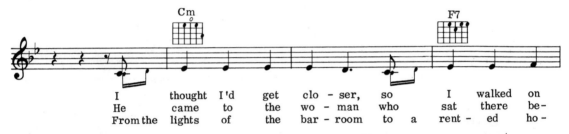

I thought I'd get clo - ser, so I walked on
He came to the wo - man who sat there be -
From the lights of the bar - room to a rent - ed ho -

ov - er, I sat down and asked her her name.
side me, He had a strange look on his face.
tel room, we walked with - out talk - ing at all.

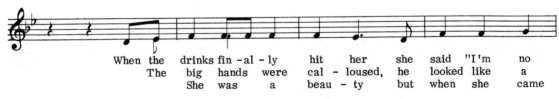

When the drinks fin - al - ly hit her she said "I'm no
The big hands were cal - loused, he looked like a
She was a beau - ty but when she came

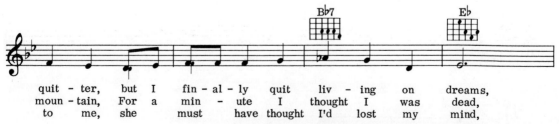

quit - ter, but I fin - al - ly quit liv - ing on dreams,
moun - tain, For a min - ute I thought I was dead,
to me, she must have thought I'd lost my mind,

64
I Walk The Line

Words & Music **Johnny Cash**

Moderately bright

(no chord)   C7   F

I keep a   close watch   on this heart of   mine.____
very, very   eas-y   to be   true.____

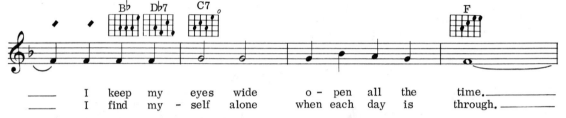

Bb Db7 C7   F

____ I keep my eyes   wide   o-pen all the   time.____
____ I find my-self alone   when each day is   through. ____

F7   Bb   F

____ I keep the ends out   for the tie that   binds.____ } Be-cause you're
____ Yes, I'll ad-mit that   I'm a fool for   you.____

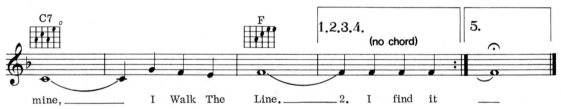

C7   F   1.2.3.4.   5.
                    (no chord)

mine,____   I Walk The   Line.____ 2. I find it   ____

3. As sure as night is dark and day is light,
   I keep you on my mind both day and night.
   And happiness I've known proves that it's right,
   Because you're mine, I Walk The Line.

4. You've got a way to keep me on your side,
   You give me cause for love that I can't hide.
   For you I know I'd even try to turn the tide,
   Because you're mine, I Walk The Line.

5. I keep a close watch on this heart of mine,
   I keep my eyes wide open all the time.
   I keep the ends out for the tie that binds,
   Because you're mine, I Walk The Line.

BALLAD

65
The Last Thing On My Mind

Words & Music **Tom Paxton**

It's a les-son too late for the learn-ing, Made of sand, made of
rea-son a-plen-ty for go-ing, This I know, this I
lie in my bed in the morn-ing With-out you, with-out

sand. In the wink of an eye my soul is turn-ing ___ In your
know, For the weeds have been stead-i ly grow-ing. ___ Please don't
you. Each song in my breast dies a-born-ing ___ With-out

hand, in your hand.
go, please don't go. } Are you go - ing a-way ___ with no
you, with-out you.

word of fare-well, Will there be not a trace ___ left be-hind? ___ Well I

could have loved ___ you bet-ter, did-n't mean to be un-kind, ___ You know

that was the last ___ thing on ___ my mind. 2. You've got
3. As I

mind, That was the last ___ thing on my mind.

EASY 1

66
Leaving On A Jet Plane

Words & Music **John Denver**

Moderato

Verse

1. All my bags are packed, __ I'm read-y to go, I'm
(2. There's so) man - y times __ I've let you down, So
(3. _____) Now the time __ has come to leave you,

stand - ing here __ out - side your door, __ I hate to wake __ you
man - y times __ I've played a - round, __ I tell you now __
one more time, __ let me kiss you, __ Then close your eyes, __

up to say __ good - bye
they don't mean __ a - thing.   But the
I'll be on __ my way   Ev - 'ry

dawn is break - in', it's ear - ly morn, __ The
place I go __ I'll think of you. __ Ev - 'ry
Dream a - bout __ the days to come, __ When

tax - i's wait-in', he's blow-in' his horn. __ Al - read - y I'm so
song I sing __ I'll sing for you. __ When I come back I'll
I won't have __ to leave a - lone. __ A - bout the times __

67
Long Black Veil

Words & Music **Marijohn Wilkin & Danny Dill**

Ten years a-go,___ on a cold dark night,___ there was some-one

killed 'neath the town hall light.___ There were few at the scene, but

they all a-greed that the slay-er who ran looked a lot like

me.___ The judge said "Son, what is your al-i-

scaf-fold was high___ and e-ter-ni-ty

-bi?___ If you were some-where else, then you won't have to die." I

near,___ She stood in the crowd and shed___ not a tear.___ But

spoke not a word,___ tho' it meant my life, for I had been in the

some-times at night,___ when the cold wind___ moans,___ in a long black

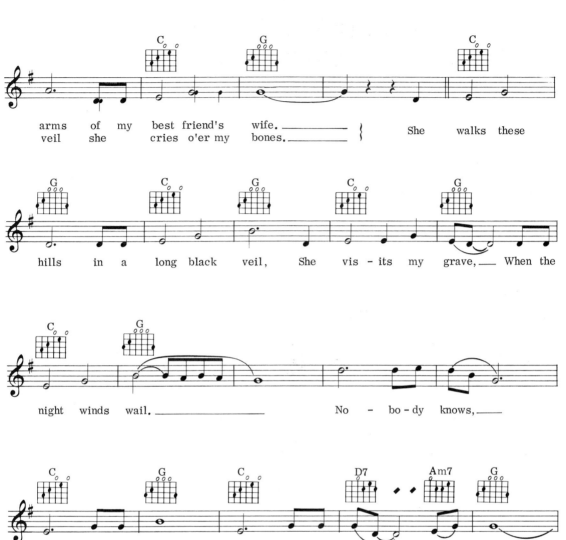

arms of my best friend's wife. _____ } She walks these
veil she cries o'er my bones. _____

hills in a long black veil, She vis - its my grave, ___ When the

night winds wail. _____ No - bo - dy knows, ___

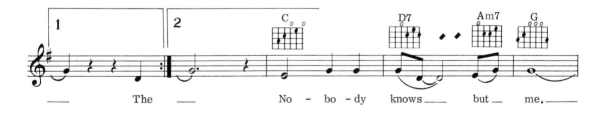

No - bo - dy sees, No - bo - dy knows ___ but ___ me. ___

1   2

___ The ___ No - bo - dy knows ___ but ___ me.

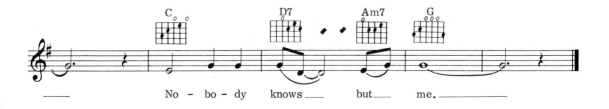

___ No - bo - dy knows ___ but ___ me. _____

70, Pop

68
A Loser With Nothing To Lose

Words & Music **Kris Kristofferson**

All my
(2. No more

tears _____ have been cried, All my heart-aches _____ have
so - row, _____ no pride, No more feel - ings _____ to

died, Leav - ing noth-ing, _____ not e - ven _____ the blues.
hide; they were gone _____ not too long _____ af - ter you.

All I cared for _____ is gone, I won't care _____ from now
Noth - ing hurts _____ an - y more, noth - ing's worth _____ cry - ing

on. } I'm A Los - er, _____ with noth - ing _____ to lose. _____
for. }

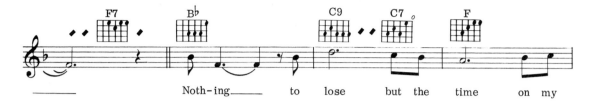

Noth-ing_____ to lose but the time on my

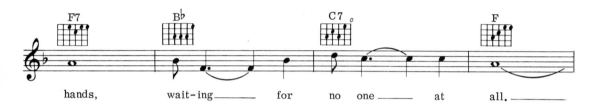

hands, wait-ing_____ for no one _____ at all. _____

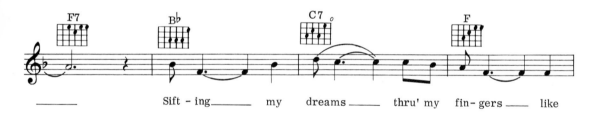

_____ Sift - ing_____ my dreams _____ thru' my fin - gers ___ like

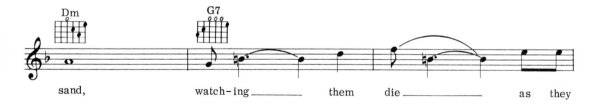

sand, watch-ing_____ them die _____ as they

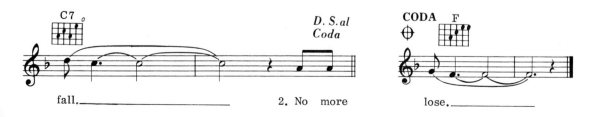

fall._____ 2. No more lose._____

69
A Little Bitty Tear

Words & Music **Hank Cochran**

Moderato

1. When you said you were leav-ing to-mor-row, that to-
2. I said I'd laugh when you left me, pull a
3. Ev-'ry-thing went like I planned it, and I

day was our last day. I said there'd be no
face as you went out the door. That I'd have an-oth-er one
really put on a show. I thought I was gon-na

sor-row, That I'd laugh when you walked a-way.
wait-ing, To wave good-bye as you go.
stand it, But when you got to the door.

a tempo

1. But
2. But } A Lit-tle Bit-ty Tear let me down,
3. Then

Spoiled my act as a clown; I had it made up not to make a

frown; Oh, but A Lit-tle Bit-ty Tear let me down.

D. C.

Make The World Go Away

Words & Music **Hank Cochran**

1. Do you re-member when you loved me, ____ Be-fore the world took me a-stray. ____ If you do, then for-give me, ____ And Make The World ____ Go A - way. ____ Make The World Go A-

hurt you, ____ I'll make it up ____ day by day. ____ Just say you love me like you used to, ____ And Make The World ____ Go A - way. ____

CHORUS
way. ____ And get it off ____ my ____ shoul - ders. ____ Say the things you used to say, ____ And Make The World ____ Go A - way. ____ Make The World Go A-

way. ____ 2. I'm sor-ry if I - way. ____

Mammas Don't Let Your Babies Grow Up To Be Cowboys

Words & Music **Ed Bruce & Patsy Bruce**

Moderato ♩ = 63

mp

Cow-boys ain't eas - y to love, and they're hard - er to
Cow-boys like smok - y old pool rooms and clear moun - tain

hold.
Morn - ings.

They'd rath-er
Lit - tle warm

give you a song than dia - monds or gold.
pup - ies and chil - dren and girls of the night.

Lone Star belt buck-les___ and old fad - ed Le - vis and
Them that don't know him___ won't like him and them that do

each night be - gins___ a new day. If you don't un - der-
some-times won't know how to___ take him. He ain't wrong, he's just

stand him and he don't die___ young; He'll prob - 'ly just ride___ a-
dif - f'rent, his pride___ won't__ let him do things to make you think___ he's

72

STRAITS
COUNTRY STRUMMING
THIS
O/T 3

Me And Bobby McGee

Words & Music **Kris Kristofferson & Fred Foster**

Busted flat in Baton Rouge; Headin' for the
coal mines of Kentucky to the California

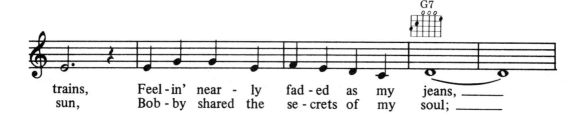

trains, Feelin' nearly faded as my jeans, ____
sun, Bobby shared the secrets of my soul; ____

Bobby thumbed a diesel down ____ just before it rained;
Standin' right beside me, Lord, through everything I done,

Took us all the way to New Orleans, ____
And every night she kept me from the cold; ____ Then

I took my harpoon out of my dirty, red bandanna and was
somewhere near Salinas, Lord, I let her slip away

blowin' sad, while Bobby sang the blues; ____ With them
lookin' for the home I hope she'll find; ____ And I'd trade

73
The Moon's A Harsh Mistress

Words & Music **Jimmy Webb**

1. See her how she flies _____ gold-en sails a-cross the
2. Once the sun did shine _____ Lord, it felt so

sky _____ Close e-nough to touch _____
fine _____ The moon a phan-tom rose _____

But care-ful if you try _____ though she looks as warm as
Thru the moun-tains and the pines _____ and then the dark-ness

gold The moon's a harsh mis-tress _____
fell The moon's a harsh mis-tress _____

the moon can be so cold. _____
it's hard to love her well. _____

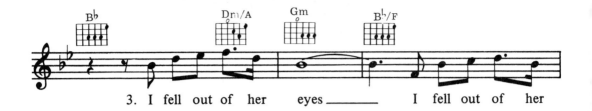

3. I fell out of her   eyes _____   I fell out of her

heart   I fell down on my   face____

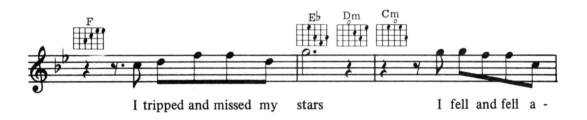

I tripped and missed my   stars   I fell and fell a -

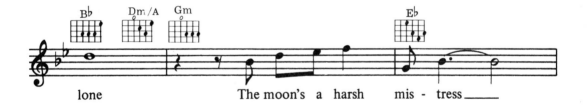

lone   The moon's a harsh   mis - tress _____

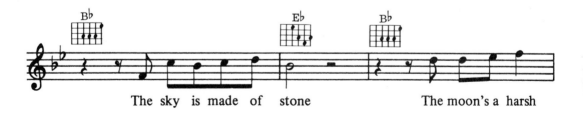

The sky is made of   stone   The moon's a harsh

mis - tress ____   She's hard to call your   own. _____

74
One Day At A Time

Words & Music **Marijohn Wilkin & Kris Kristofferson**

CHORUS

take one day at a time._____ } One

take one day at a time._____

day at a time, _____ Sweet Je - sus, _____ that's all I'm

ask - ing from you. _____ Just give me the strength to

do ev - 'ry day what I have to do._____

Yes - ter - day's gone, _____ Sweet Je - sus, _____ and to-

-mor - row may nev - er be mine._____ Lord,

help me to - day, show me the way, One day at a

1
time._____

2
time._____

Paper Roses

Words **Janice Torre**
Music **Fred Spielman**

Ring Of Fire

Words & Music **Merle Kilgore & June Carter**

Moderately bright

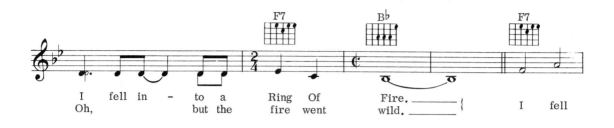

I fell in - to a Ring Of Fire. _____
Oh, but the fire went wild. _____

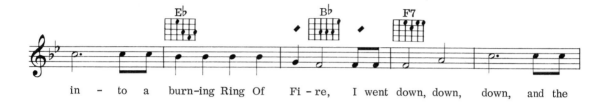

I fell in - to a burn-ing Ring Of Fi - re, I went down, down, down, and the

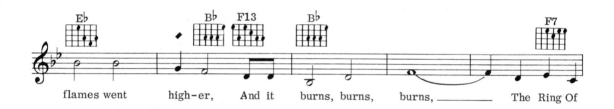

flames went high-er, And it burns, burns, burns, _____ The Ring Of

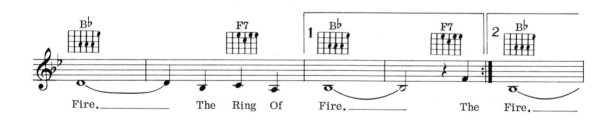

Fire. _____ The Ring Of Fire. _____ The Fire. _____

_____ And it burns, burns, burns, _____ The Ring Of

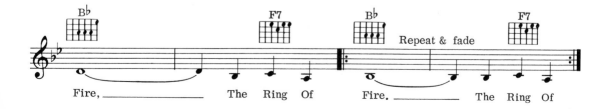

Fire, _____ The Ring Of Fire. _____ The Ring Of

77
Polk Salad Annie

Words & Music **Tony Joe White**

chain gang   (A mean vicious woman)

2. Every day 'fore supper time, she'd go down by the truck patch,
   And pick her a mess o' polk salad and carry it home in a towsack;
   Polk Salad Annie, 'gators got your granny,
   Everybody said it was a shame,
   'Cause her mama was a workin' on the chain gang.
   A wretched, spiteful, straight-razor tottin' woman;
   Lord have mercy, pick a mess of it.

3. Her daddy was lazy and no count, claimed he had a bad back,
   All her brothers were fit for was stealin' watermelons out of my truck patch;
   Polk Salad Annie, the 'gators got your granny,
   Everybody said it was a shame,
   'Cause her mama was workin' on the chain gang.
   (Sock a little polk salad to me, you know I need me a mess of it.)

78
Tennessee Waltz

Words & Music **Redd Stewart & Pee Wee King**

79
Sixteen Tons

Words & Music **Merle Travis**

Moderato

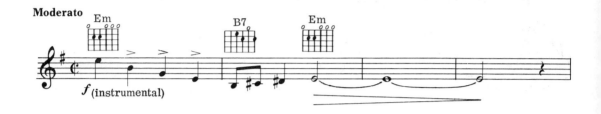

f (instrumental)

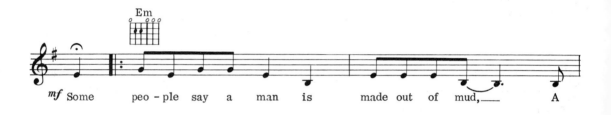

mf Some peo-ple say a man is made out of mud,___ A

poor man's made out of mus-cle and blood, Mus-cle and blood and

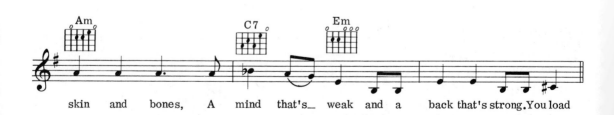

skin and bones, A mind that's_ weak and a back that's strong. You load

CHORUS

Six - teen Tons, what do you get?__ An - oth -er day old-er and

deep-er in debt.__ Say broth-er don't you call me, 'cause I can't go;__ I

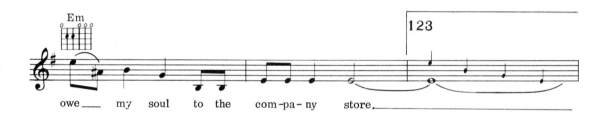

owe __ my soul to the com -pa- ny store.__

2. I was __

2. I was born one mornin' when the sun didn't shine,
   I picked up my shovel and I walked to the mine,
   I loaded Sixteen Tons of number nine coal,
   And the straw boss said "Well bless my soul."
       (Chorus)

3. I was born one mornin', it was drizzling rain,
   Fightin' and trouble are my middle name,
   I was raised in a cane-brake by an ole mama lion,
   Cain't no hightoned woman make me walk the line.
       (Chorus)

4. If you see me comin', better step aside,
   A lotta men didn't, a lotta men died,
   One fist of iron, the other of steel,
   If the right don't get you, then the left one will.
       (Chorus)

80
She Believes In Me

Words & Music **Steve Gibb**

She Thinks I Still Care

Words & Music **Dicky Lee**

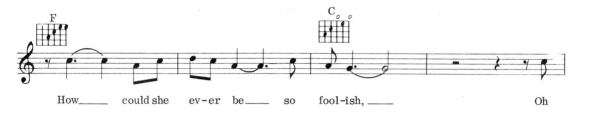

How___ could she ev-er be___ so fool-ish, ___ Oh

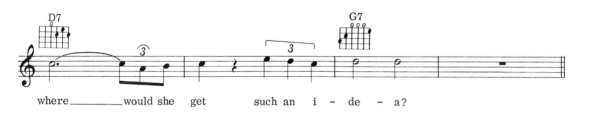

where_____would she get such an i - de - a?

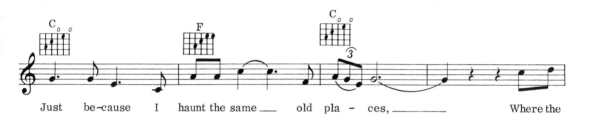

Just be-cause I haunt the same ___ old pla - ces, _____ Where the

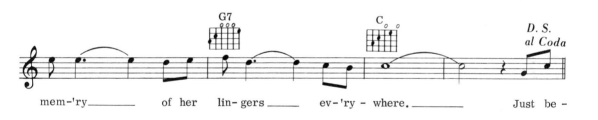

mem-'ry_____ of her lin-gers _____ ev-'ry - where. _____ Just be -

Just be - cause I saw her then went all to piec - es, _____

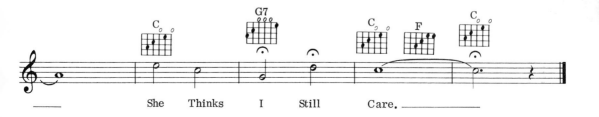

_____ She Thinks I Still Care. _____

82
Single Girl

Words & Music **Martha Sharp**

Moderato

The
I'm a { Sin - gle___ Girl, ___

all a-lone___ in a great big town; ___ The Sin-gle___ Girl, ___
won-drin'if love___ could be pass-in' me by; ___ I'm a Sin-gle___ Girl, ___ and

gets so___ tired___ of love let-tin' her down; _____ The life's un-real___ and the
I know___ all ___ a - bout men and their lies. _____ Nobod-y loves___ me 'cos

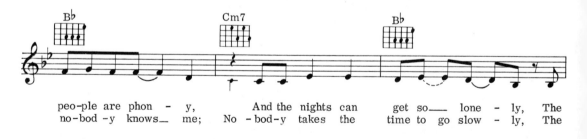

peo-ple are phon - y, And the nights can get so___ lone - ly, The
no-bod -y knows___ me; No - bod-y takes the time to go slow - ly, The

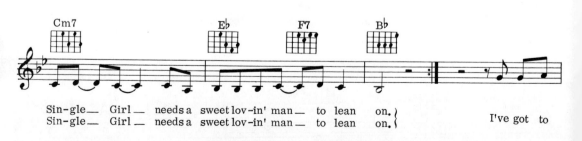

Sin-gle___ Girl ___ needs a sweet lov-in' man ___ to lean on. }
Sin-gle___ Girl ___ needs a sweet lov-in' man ___ to lean on. }

I've got to

83
Some Days Are Diamonds
(Some Days Are Stone)

Words & Music **Dick Feller**

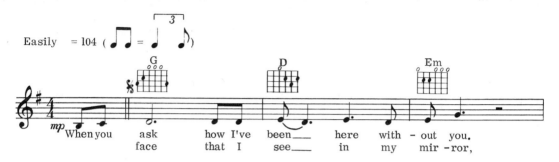

When you ask how I've been here with-out you.
face that I see in my mir-ror,

I'd like to say I've been fine, And I do;
more and more, is a stran-ger to me;

But we both know the truth is hard to come by,
More and more, I can see there's a dan-ger

And if I told the truth, that's not quite true.}
in be-com-ing what I nev-er thought I'd be. {

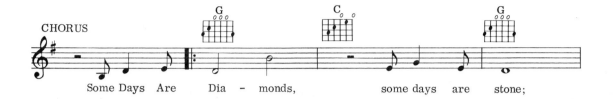

CHORUS

Some Days Are Dia - monds, some days are stone;

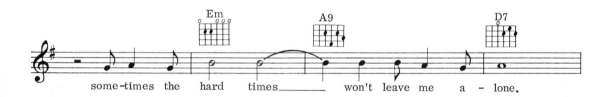

some-times the hard times_____ won't leave me a - lone.

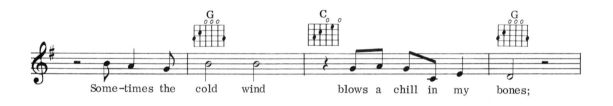

Some-times the cold wind blows a chill in my bones;

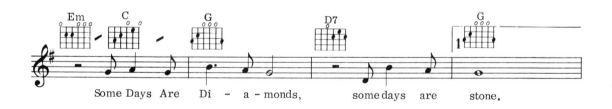

Some Days Are Di - a - monds, some days are stone.

Now the stone. Some Days Are

84
Step By Step

Words & Music **Eddie Rabbit, Even Stevens & David Malloy**

Moderato
Verses

1. She seems a mil – lion miles a - way

When she walks by you don't know what to say

You're gon-na make a move, you bet-ter make it now

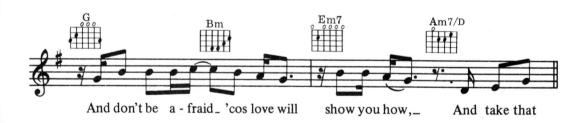

And don't be a - fraid 'cos love will show you how, And take that

CHORUS

First step, ask her out and treat her like a la - dy

2. She looks too beautiful to touch,
   But your heart keeps talking to you,
   "Now don't give up"
   You think you see something in her eyes,
   But you will never know until you try,
   But you've gotta take that.   (Chorus)

85
Sunday Morning Comin' Down

Words & Music **Kris Kristofferson**

Well, I woke up Sun-day morn-in' with no
smoked my brain the night be-fore with

way to hold my head that did-n't hurt; ___ And the
cig-a-rette and songs that I'd been a-pick-in; But I

beer I had for break-fast was-n't bad, so I had one more for des-
lit my first and watched a small kid cuss-in' at a can that he was

sert; _____ Then I fum-bled through my clos-et for my
kick-in'; _____ Then I crossed the emp-ty street and caught the

clothes and found my clean-est ___ dir-ty shirt; ___ And I
Sun-day smell of some-one ___ fry-in' chick-en; And it

shaved my face, and combed my hair, and stum-bled down the stair to meet the

In the park I saw a daddy with a laughing little girl that he was swingin',
And I stopped beside a sunday school and listened to the song that they were singin',
Then I headed back for home, and somewhere far away a lonely bell was ringin',
And it echoed thru the canyon like the disappearing dreams of yesterday. (Chorus)

86
Take Me Home, Country Roads

Words & Music **Bill Danoff, Taffy Nivert & John Denver**

87
That Old Time Feelin'

Words & Music **Baker Knight**

sor-ry but__ it took me_____ by sur - prise,_____ To be
look-in' at ___ the fool who____ used to be, _____ In an-

look-ing in those old ___ fam-il-iar eyes._____ If I'm
oth-er world where love___ was new to me._____ But I

act-in' fun-ny please don't turn a - way._____ See-ing
learned my les-son when I let you go._____ And there's

you has brought me back___ to yes-ter-day. Yes, you're
one thing that I've want - ed you to know.

If That Old Time Feel-in' e - ver__ starts a - gain,_____

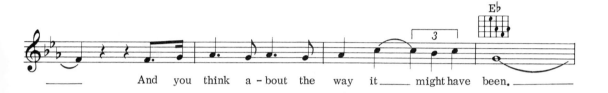

_____ And you think a - bout the way it____ might have been._____

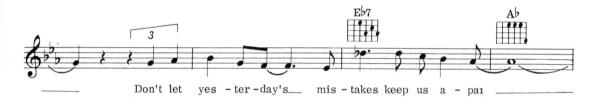

_____ Don't let yes - ter - day's__ mis - takes keep us a - par _____

_____ 'Cause That Old Time Feel-in's still in - side my heart.

rubato

If that Old Time Feel-in's still in - side my heart._____

88
Talking In Your Sleep

Words & Music **Roger Cook & Bobby Wood**

89
There Goes My Everything

Words & Music **Dallas Frazier**

90

Tobacco Road

Words & Music **John D. Loudermilk**

I was born in a dump,— Ma-ma died,_____ and
Gon-na leave_____ get a job,—— With the help,— and the

dad-dy got drunk. Left me here— to die or grow,—
grace from a-bove, Save some money, get rich I know,—

In the mid-dle of To-bac-co Road._____ Wo, wo, wo;___
Bring it back — to To-bac-co Road._____ Wo, wo, wo;___

Grew up in___ a rust-y shack,— All I had was
Bring dy-na-mite, and a crane,— Blow it up, start all

hang-in' on my back, On-ly you___ know how I loathe___
ov-er a-gain, Build a town___ be proud to show,—

This place called To - bac - co Road._____ But it's home,___
Give the name _____ To - bac - co Road._____ But it's home,___

___ The on - ly life I've___ ev - er

known. On - ly you _____ know how I
I des - pise _____ you 'cos you're

loathe._____ To - bac - co
filth - y;___ But I love___ you, 'cos you're home.\-

Road.

Repeat & fade

(Repeat & fade)

91
Together We Are Beautiful

Words & Music **Ken Leray**

Try A Little Tenderness

Words & Music Harry Woods, Jimmy Campbell & Reg Connelly

Until It's Time For You To Go

Words & Music **Buffy Sainte-Marie**

What A Difference You've Made In My Life

Words & Music **Archie Jordan**

When You're In Love With A Beautiful Woman

Words & Music **Even Stevens**

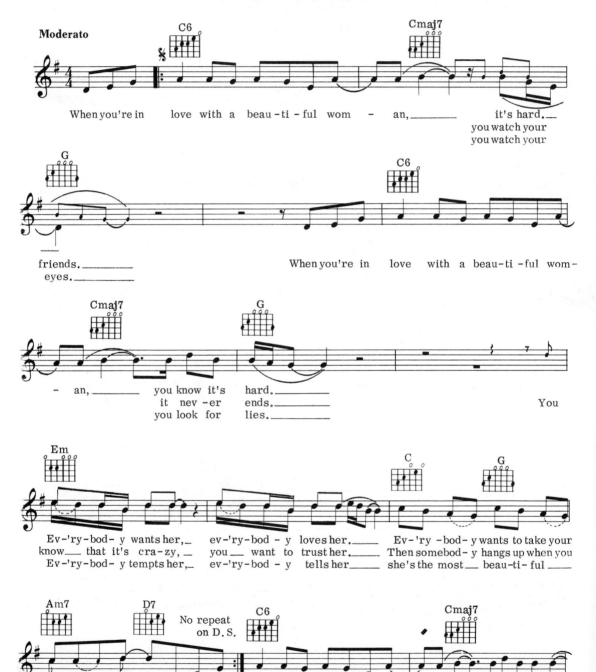

May-be it's just an e-go___ prob-lem.

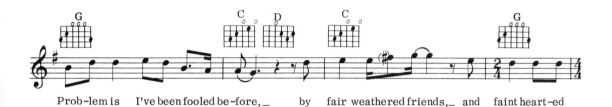

Prob-lem is I've been fooled be-fore,___ by fair weathered friends,___ and faint heart-ed

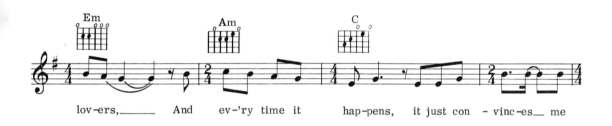

lov-ers,_____ And ev-'ry time it hap-pens, it just con - vinc-es___ me

more._____ When you're in   When you're in

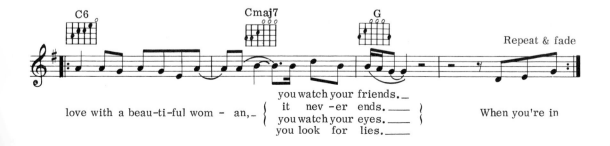

love with a beau-ti-ful wom - an,- { you watch your friends.___ }   When you're in
                                     { it nev-er ends.___ }
                                     { you watch your eyes.___ }
                                     { you look for lies.___ }

Repeat & fade

When My Blue Moon Turns To Gold Again

Words & Music **Wiley Walker & Gene Sullivan**

Wichita Lineman

Words & Music **Jim Webb**

Repeat and Fade

98
Will The Circle Be Unbroken

Traditional

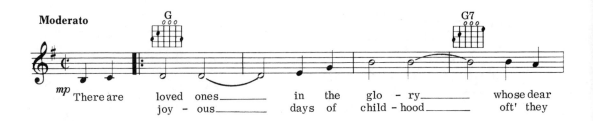

There are loved ones___ in the glo - ry___ whose dear
joy - ous___ days of child - hood___ oft' they

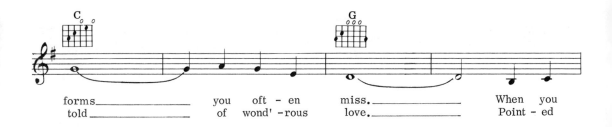

forms___ you oft - en miss.___ When you
told___ of wond' -rous love.___ Point - ed

close your___ earth - ly sto - ry___ will you
to the___ dy - ing Sav - ior,___ now they

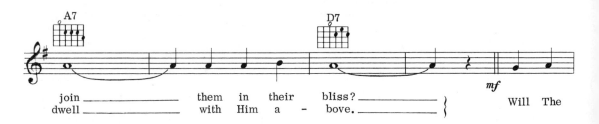

join___ them in their bliss?___ Will The
dwell___ with Him a - bove.___

Cir - cle___ Be Un - bro - ken, ___ by and

99
You Light Up My Life

Words & Music **Joe Brooks**

Moderato

So man - y nights, I'd sit by my
Rol - lin' at sea, a - drift on the

win - dow, wait - ing for some-one___ to sing me his
wa - ters, could it be fi - n'lly___ I'm turn - ing for

song. So man - y dreams I kept deep in -
home. Fi - n'lly a chance to say, "Hey! I

- side me, a - lone in the dark, but now you've come a -
love you." Nev - er a - gain to be all a -

- long.
- lone. And you light up my life.

You give me hope, to car - ry on. You

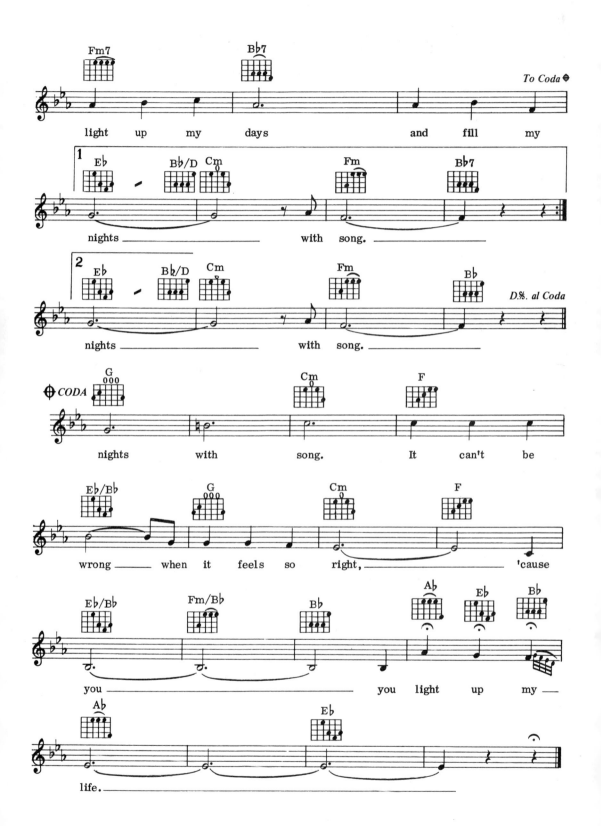

100
The Wonder Of You

Words & Music **Baker Knight**

Slowly, with feeling

1 When no - one else can un - der - stand me,
2 And when you smile, the world is bright - er.
3 You'll nev - er know how much I love you.

When ev' - ry - thing I do is wrong, You give me love and con - so -
You touch my hand and I'm a king. Your kiss to me is worth a
My love is yours and yours a - lone, And it's so won - der - ful to

la - tion. You give me hope to car - ry on, And you try to show your
for - tune. Your love to me is ev' - ry - thing, And you're al - ways there to
have you, To have you for my ver - y own. Guess I'll nev - er know the

love for me in ev' - ry - thing you do. ⎫ That's the won - der,
lend a hand in all I try to do. ⎬
rea - son why you love me as you do. ⎭

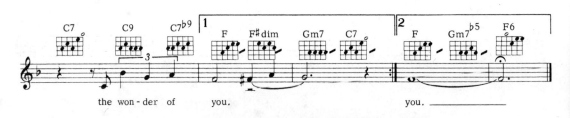

the won - der of you.   you. _____

101
You're The Devil In Disguise

Words & Music **Bill Giant, Bernie Baum & Florence Kaye**

You look like an an - gel, _____ Walk like an an - gel,___

Talk like an an - gel, _____ but I got wise;

(tacet - - - - -)

You're the dev-il in dis - guise. Oh, yes, you are, ___ dev - il in dis-

To Coda ⊕

-guise. Mm. ___ You fooled me ___ with your kiss - es

I thought that ___ I was in heav - en

You cheat - ed and you schemed, _____ Heav-en knows___ how you

But I was sure sur - prised, _____ Heav-en help ___ me, I

D.%. al Coda

lied to me, _____ You're not the way you seemed. } You

did - n't see ___ the dev - il in your eyes.

⊕ CODA

Repeat to fade

_____ Dev - il in dis - guise, _____ Oh, yes, you are, Dev - il in dis-

4/01(40160)

New from Music Sales - the one-and only, ultimate busker book! It's *the* book to take to a party... to a gig... on your holiday... or to that famous desert island!

It's packed with literally hundreds and hundreds of the best-loved songs of all time... from vintage standards of the 30s right through to the latest pop hits.

"The Suitcase Book"!

"Probably the best songbook in the world."

The Busker's Fake Book 1001 All-Time Hit Songs

"The only songbook you'll ever need!"

For piano, organ, guitar, all electronic keyboards and all 'C' instruments. With an easy-to-use A-Z title finder plus a classified 'song type' index.
As a taster, here's just a quarter of the titles in this unique bumper songbook ...

'A' You're Adorable
A Fine Romance
A Fool Such As I
A Hard Day's Night
A Man And A Woman
A Teenager In Love
Act Naturally
Against All Odds
Ain't Misbehavin'
All I Have To Do Is Dream
All My Loving
America
An American In Paris
An Old Fashioned Love Song
Angel Eyes
Another Suitcase In Another Hall
As Time Goes By
Band On The Run
Barbara Ann
Baubles Bangles And Beads
Because
Bennie And The Jets
Big Girls Don't Cry
Big Spender
Bird Dog
Blowin' In The Wind
Boogie Woogie Bugle Boy
Buffalo Gals
Bye Bye Love
California Dreaming
Can't Smile Without You
Candle In The Wind
Caravan
Chantilly Lace
Come Fly With Me
Consider Yourself
Crazy
Cruising Down The River
Dancing Queen
Daniel
Desafinado
Devil In Disguise
Diamonds Are A Girl's Best Friend
Do You Know The Way To San Jose
Don't Cry For Me Argentina
Don't Pay The Ferryman
Don't Sleep In The Subway
East Enders
Ebony And Ivory
Eleanor Rigby
Empty Chairs At Empty Tables
The Entertainer
Every Breath You Take
First Time Ever I Saw Your Face
Fools Rush In
From Me To You
Funiculi, Funicula
Für Elise
Get Back
Get It On (Bang A Gong)
The Girl From Ipanema
Good Vibrations
Goodbye Yellow Brick Road
Guys And Dolls
Happy Xmas (War Is Over)
Havah Nagilah
He Ain't Heavy He's My Brother
Hello Mary Lou

Hello, Goodbye
Here, There And Everywhere
Hey Jude
Hey, Good Lookin'
Honeysuckle Rose
I Came I Saw I Conga'd
I Don't Want To Spoil The Party
I Dreamed A Dream
I Feel Pretty
I Fought The Law
I Left My Heart In San Francisco
I Saw Her Standing There
I'm A Loser
I'm Beginning To See The Light
I'm Still Standing
If I Had A Hammer
If I Were A Bell
In The Air Tonight
It Never Rains In Southern California
It's Not Unusual
It's So Easy
Jambalaya
Jealous Guy
La Ronde De l'Amour
Lady D'Arbanville
The Lady Is Red
The Lambeth Walk
The Last Time I Saw Paris
Layla
Leaning On A Lamp Post
Let It Be
Let's Twist Again
The Lion Sleeps Tonight
Live And Let Die
Long Tall Sally
Love And Marriage
Lover Man
Lucille
Luck Be A Lady
Lullaby Of Birdland
Maple Leaf Rag
Maria
Me And My Girl
Mister Bojangles
Money For Nothing
Mull Of Kintyre
Never On A Sunday
Nights In White Satin
Norwegian Wood
Not Fade Away
O Sole Mio
Oh Pretty Woman
Ol' Man River
Old Shep
On A Slow Boat To China
Only The Lonely
P.S. I Love You
Peggy Sue
Pennies From Heaven
Penny Lane
Pigalle
Poison Ivy
The Power Of Love
Raindrops Keep Falling On My Head
Rave On
Rhapsody In Blue
Riders On The Storm
Rock Around The Clock

Ruby Don't Take Your Love To Town
Satin Doll
Scarborough Fair
Shake Rattle And Roll
She Loves You
Singing The Blues
Sixteen Tons
Sloop John B
Smoke Gets In Your Eyes
Solitude
Something
Somewhere
Spanish Eyes
Standing On The Corner
Stars Fell On Alabama
Stranger In Paradise
Strangers In The Night
Streets Of London
Sugarbush
Suitcase Of Swing
Summertime Blues
Sunshine Of Your Love
Sweet Charity
Swing Low, Sweet Chariot
Take Back Your Mink
Take That Look Off Your Face
Take The 'A' Train
Teen Angel
The Tender Trap
That'll Be The Day
Theme For A Dream
These Foolish Things
They Didn't Believe Me
This Guy's In Love With You
This Land Is Your Land
These Were The Days
Three Little Fishies
Till There Was You
To Know Him Is To Love Him
Tonight
True Love Ways
Tulips From Amsterdam
Tutti Frutti
Unchained Melody
Under The Boardwalk
Up, Up And Away
Uptown Girl
The Very Thought Of You
Wake Up Little Susie
Walk Tall
The Way You Look Tonight
We Can Work It Out
We Don't Need Another Hero
We Shall Overcome
We'll Meet Again
What Kind Of Fool Am I
Wheels
When I'm Sixty Four
When Irish Eyes Are Smiling
When This Lousy War Is Over
Where Have All The Flowers Gone
Witchcraft
With A Little Help From My Friends
Woman
Yellow Submarine
Yesterday
Your Cheatin' Heart
Your Song

Melody, lyrics and guitar chords to literally hundreds and hundreds of the best songs of all time... from the golden standards through to the great pop hits of today.

While compiling this huge book, editor/arranger Peter Lavender kept all the artwork in a huge suitca But now that it's printed, this new mega-bumper bu book is a lot easier to carry around!

Surprisingly portable, in fact, at the usual songbook of 12" x 9"... with some 656 pages!

As well as the 1,001 songs, the book includes a ha A-Z alphabetical title index *and* a classified index, to

Hundreds More Hits For Buskers!

All the songs people love to hear - and sing.

More than a dozen books of all-time hits (with great new titles being added all the time) ...

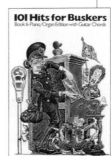

101 Hits for Buskers, Book 3
Piano/Organ/Guitar
AM25099

101 Hits for Buskers, Book 4
Piano/Organ/Guitar
AM26550

101 Hits for Buskers, Book 12
Piano/Organ/Guitar
AM79765

Hits for Buskers, 2
/Organ/Guitar
9803

101 Hits for Buskers, Book 2
Bb Edition
AM19811

101 Hits for Buskers, Book 11
Piano/Organ/Guitar
AM77306

101 Hits for Buskers, Book 13
Piano/Organ/Guitar
AM84062

Hits for Buskers, 1
/Organ/Guitar
7229

101 Hits for Buskers, Book 9
Piano/Organ/Guitar
AM66366

101 Hits for Buskers, Book 10
Piano/Organ/Guitar
AM66440

101 Hits for Buskers, Book 7
Piano/Organ/Guitar
AM33654

101 Hits for Buskers, Book 8
Piano/Organ/Guitar
AM36914

101 Hits for Buskers, Book 5
Piano/Organ/Guitar
AM29570

101 Hits for Buskers, Book 6
Piano/Organ/Guitar
AM29869

Bringing you the world's best music.

The Beatles

Enya

Phil Collins

Van Morrison

Bob Dylan

Sting

Paul Simon

Tracy Chapman

Eric Clapton

Pink Floyd

New Kids On The Block

Bryan Adams

Tina Turner

Elton John

Bee Gees

Whitney Houston

AC/DC

Bringing you the
words

**All the latest in rock and pop.
Plus the brightest and best in West
End show scores. Music books for
every instrument under the sun.
And exciting new teach-yourself
ideas like "Let's Play Keyboard" -
in cassette/book packs, or on video.
Available from all good music shops.**

and
music

**Music Sales' complete
catalogue lists thousands of
titles and is available free
from your local music shop,
or direct from Music Sales
Limited. Please send a
cheque or postal order for
£1.50 (for postage) to:**

Buddy

Five Guys Named Moe

Les Misérables

West Side Story

Phantom Of The Opera

Show Boat

The Rocky Horror Show

Music Sales Limited
Newmarket Road,
Bury St Edmunds,
Suffolk IP33 3YB

**Bringing you the
world's best music.**

Night ___ falls so soft ___ on the dead and hard on the liv - ing,

si - lent and still, ___ where we lay. ___ Oh, ___

___ God, pro - tect us, the chil - dren of a mis - un -der stand -ing

vic - tims of games ___ peo - ple play. ___ Hold

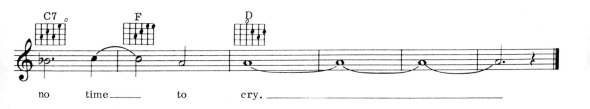

on, boy, don't lose your mind. ___ Hold on, boy, it's

no time ___ to cry. ___